10 BEST SHAKESPEARE STORIES EVER!

Terry Deary

Author of Horrible Histories

SCHOLASTIC

For the real Edward Allen.

Scholastic Children's Books,
Euston House, 24 Eversholt Street,
London, NW1 1DB, UK

A division of Scholastic Ltd
London ~ New York ~ Toronto ~ Sydney ~ Auckland

First published in the UK under the title *Top Ten*
by Scholastic Ltd, 1998
This edition published 2009

Text copyright © Terry Deary, 1998
Illustrations copyright © Michael Tickner, 1998

All rights reserved

10 digit ISBN 1 407 10819 0
13 digit ISBN 978 1407 10819 3

Printed and bound by CPI Bookmarque, Croydon, CR0 4TD

10 9 8 7

The right of Terry Deary and Michael Tickner to be identified as the author and
illustrator of this work respectively has been asserted by them in accordance with
the Copyright, Designs and Patents Act, 1988.

CONTENTS

INTRODUCTION

William Shakespeare wrote plays. He didn't write them just for pupils to read in school or for teachers to use for impossible exam questions. Let's get this straight:

> Shakespeare wrote plays so people would be entertained. He wanted people to have FUN!

And when Queen Elizabeth I and King James I were ruling Britain people *did* have fun watching performances of Shakespeare's plays. The plays were, and still are, every bit as entertaining as today's television soap operas. They have…

- death and destruction
- jokes and jests
- weird witchcraft
- rogues and royals
- hatred and heartache
- blood and butchery

7

Everything for all round entertainment. But above all they have great stories and terrific characters. There are scenes to make you laugh and scenes to make you cry ... often within the same play.

So, here they are. The ten plays selected here are the ones that have been performed most over the past 150 years. *The ten best Shakespeare plays ever!*

They've been re-told in a way you are more familiar with, using modern language and modern styles, from a photo-love-story to a newspaper report. Then there are the fascinating facts about Shakespeare, his life and the different ways in which his plays have been performed.

Remember:

> This book has been written so you will be entertained. When you read it you should have FUN!

STORY 1: A MIDSUMMER NIGHT'S DREAM

Our first story is a play written around 1595 when Queen Elizabeth I was on the throne and Sir Walter Raleigh was off to what is now Guyana in South America on an expedition to find the legendary city of gold – El Dorado! He failed to find it – probably because it doesn't exist. But he was typical of many Elizabethan sailors and explorers who believed that wonderful lands and riches lay across the oceans ... full of strange and bewitching creatures.

The Elizabethans believed in witches and spirits and these made great material for a playwright like Shakespeare.

Shakespeare's plays are usually divided into three types – Comedies, Tragedies and History plays. Then there are some that are a bit of each, and that makes it a *problem* to stick a label on them … so writers usually call them "Problem" plays!

A *Midsummer Night's Dream* is a *comedy*. That doesn't mean it's a laugh a minute – though it does have some funny scenes – it really means that everything turns out well in the end.

Here the play is re-told by one of the spirit characters, called Puck. Actually "Puck" was an Elizabethan name for any mischievous spirit and in some parts of Britain they called them by the name "Puke"! The story is fast-moving and involves lots of crazy mix-ups and magic…

NIGHTMARE IN ELM TREES

I'm a faerie.

Go on, then. Laugh! Giggle, smirk, snigger, chortle, chuckle, titter. Everybody else does. They think fairies are little girls with half a frock, a wand and a pair of wings.

How would they know? They can't even spell the faerie name!

So, let's get this right from the start. We are NOT midget moppets in mini-skirts.

Faeries are spirits, made of air, and we can take any shape we want. If I want to appear as the bully boy in big brown boots (size twelve) that haunts your dreams, then I will. And if I want to appear as a hairy spider that crawls into your left nostril while you're asleep, then I will do that too.

See! You're not laughing now, are you? Once you fall asleep you are in my world and in my power. So just be careful how you speak to me. I'm important. I have power – the power to do good or the power to do mischief, depending on who you are, of course.

In the graveyard hours of the night, owls hoot, dogs howl, ghosts moan ... and you fall asleep. That's when you enter *my* world and I enter *your* mind. I'm the lord of the dream world and you are my slaves.

My name is Robin Goodfellow – some call me Puck – and I live in the "Otherworld", that secret place beyond your Earth, where you can only go in dreams. There are a lot of woods in our Otherworld. Dark forests with twisted trees to trip you up as you try to escape from some gigantic monster with huge teeth ... that'll probably be me in one of my disguises.

Don't worry, you'll wake up before I catch you. That's all part of the game!

But it hasn't always been that way. Once, long ago, the curtain that comes between your world and mine wore thin. At certain magic times it disappeared altogether. That's when I walked into your world and humans slipped through into mine and never knew it! The real world and the dream world became all mixed up.

Midsummer Night is the most magical time of all ...

as you'll probably know if you've ever seen your dog chatting to next door's cat on the night of 21st June. The cat was me in one of my disguises.

From December till June the days grow longer. By Midsummer the daylight is at its longest and that's the time when night starts to fight back against day and the struggle tears the curtain between our worlds.

I'll tell you a story to show you what happens when your human world gets confused with my faerie world. It all happened one Midsummer Night, about two thousand years ago in Athens. It started with a quarrel as many stories do...

My lord, Oberon, the King of the Otherworld, sees his queen, Titania, with a new, young serving boy. If she were honest, Titania would admit that she stole the boy from a rich Indian king. Faeries are great thieves.

Now Oberon, being a faerie, can take any shape he likes. But he likes to take the form of a human man – one of the *ugliest* creatures Nature ever created, if you ask me. He also likes to dress up like a human king. You know the sort of thing – silk robes in rainbow colours dripping with jewels and a big gold crown.

Oberon decides he wants that young boy for his own to serve him like a slave.

So Oberon calls me to him, and plots a really rotten revenge – faeries can be rather spiteful, you know.

He sends me off to find a flower, a flower called *Love in Idleness*; he says that just one drop of juice from this flower on someone's eyelids will make them fall in love with the next thing they see.

At that moment in the forest, four young people are wandering, half-lost in the light of the pale new moon. Hermia is eloping with her love, Lysander. Helena is chasing Demetrius, begging him to marry her.

---

[1]In this story all the words in italics in speech bubbles were written by Shakespeare.

She follows him till they are too tired to walk another step. They lie down on a mossy bank and fall asleep while Oberon watches, quite invisible to human eyes. Did I mention that? Apart from changing shape, we can also make ourselves totally invisible.

When I return with the mystic juice from *Love in Idleness*, my master tells me to find Demetrius.

Sounds simple enough, doesn't it? Squirt juice on a young human's eyes so he falls in love with a young human woman. But nothing is ever that easy. Especially on a magical night like Midsummer Night.

Personally I blame Oberon for what happened next. You see, my Lord forgets to tell me that two *other* lovers are also wandering through the wood. Lysander and his wife-to-be, the lovely Hermia. Am *I* to blame if I get the wrong couple? After all, Lysander wears Athenian garments too! Anyway, I squeeze the stuff onto the eyes of young Lysander by mistake. He wakes and he sees the unloved Helena first and falls in love with her instead!

Now Lysander loves Helena, but Helena loves Demetrius, but Demetrius loves Hermia, but Hermia loves Lysander, but Lysander loves Helena, but Helena loves Demetrius, but Demetrius loves Hermia ... this circle, like a wheel, could turn and turn forever.

Then Oberon finds queen Titania lying on a grassy bank, asleep. The king puts *Love in Idleness* on her eyes, so she will love the next thing that she sees ... he does not wake her up but creeps away into the shadowy wood to watch and wait.

Let us leave the lovers for a minute. Let's look now at these six workmen wandering through the wood. Quince the carpenter, Flute the bellows mender, Robin Starveling the tailor, Snug the joiner, Snout the tinker – every one a fool. But the weaver, called Nick Bottom, is the biggest fool in all the wood … perhaps in all of Athens.

How would you like to be called Bottom? Imagine the jokes! "You're the Bottom of the class!" or "Slap his head and he becomes a smacked Bottom." You know the sort of thing. Nick Bottom suffered all that nonsense at school. No wonder he grew up a bit strange. Now, you may be wondering what these six men were doing wandering in the woods of Athens on Midsummer Night. I'm wondering that too, so I make myself invisible and watch them. It seems these six men have met to rehearse a play to entertain the Duke of Athens at his wedding party.

Nick Bottom is the bossy one. I watch him argue, fuss and try to tell the others what to do. He thinks that no one else can act but him – and, if he is allowed, Nick Bottom will play every part.

This Bottom is a blockhead, booby, dunce and clown, I think. And such an *ass* should have an ass's *head*. So I use a simple magic spell to turn the blockhead into an ass-head. Did I tell you that? Not only do we faeries have the power to change our shapes, we can also cast spells on helpless humans. So I turn boastful Bottom's head into an ass head and you should see his wailing work-mates run!

"We are haunted," old Quince cries. "Pray, masters! Fly, masters! Help!" he screams and leaves the puzzled Bottom scratching at his ass's head.

"Why do they run away?" the blockhead asks. "This is to make an ass of me," he brays and little does he know that *Puck* has made an ass of him!

I chase his foolish friends away, I change my shape and chant an ancient spell:

> Sometime a horse I'll be, sometime a hound,
> A hog, a headless bear, sometime a fire, [2]
> And neigh, and bark, and grunt, and roar, and burn,
> Like horse, hound, hog, bear, fire at every turn!

But while I chase the simple workmen something dreadful happens... Am I to blame, I ask you? I did not *see* the queen Titania lying there. She wakes. She has the flower-juice on her eyes. She'll fall in love with the next thing that she sees.

She rubs her eyes, she blinks and swoons with love.

> What angel wakes me from my flowery bed?

No angel, but the blockhead Bottom wakes her from that sleep. Now she falls in love with the weaver Nick with his ass's head and tells her young attendants:

[2]Faeries can take the form of fire. The Great Fire of London was me in one of my many disguises.

> Pluck the wings from painted butterflies
> To fan the moonbeams from his sleeping eyes!

Now Oberon is wondering if Titania is awake and what she saw when she first opened up her eyes. He calls me to him.

"My mistress with a monster is in love!" I tell him.

Oberon laughs to hear the story of Nick Bottom with the ass's head. But *then* he sees the error that I made with Demetrius. Oberon cries, "What hast thou done?" and sends me off to use the *Love in Idleness* to break that endless circle.

You remember. Helena loves Demetrius, but Demetrius loves Hermia, but Hermia loves Lysander, but Lysander loves Helena, but Helena loves Demetrius, but Demetrius loves Hermia...

Now it's almost morning; the ghosts troop home to churchyards to lie down in their wormy beds. Before morning light the lovers fall asleep. I then arrange them so that, when they wake with *Love in Idleness* on their eyes, they see the one that they're *supposed* to love.

And so it is! They wake. Now Demetrius loves Helena ... and Helena Loves Demetrius. That's sweet.

Now Hermia loves Lysander ... and Lysander loves Hermia. That's neat. They all return to Athens where they marry at the same time as their Duke.

Then Oberon releases Titania from the spell of loving ass-head Bottom while I charm his monstrous head away. (The serving boy, the cause of all the trouble, now belongs to Oberon, of course! No wonder he's so ready to forgive his queen!)

"I have had a dream," befuddled Bottom mumbles as he heads back to the city. There Bottom and his simple friends perform their play after the wedding party.

The Duke, the workmen and the lovers are all happy now and forget the nightmares in the woods. For dreams will fade when summer sun grows strong.

In the graveyard hours of the night, owls hoot, dogs howl, ghosts moan … and you fall asleep. That's when you enter *my* world and I enter *your* mind.

And on some Midsummer nights … beware. For some dreams really do come true.

Did you know…?

Ellen Terry (1848-1928), the famous actress, played the part of Puck when she was eight years old. She had come up though a trap-door at the end of the last act to give the final speech. But just as she reached the top, the man working the trap-door shut it too soon and caught her toe and broke it.

She screamed.

Her sister, who was playing Titania, ran over to her and stamped her foot on the stage to signal to the man on the trap-door to open it. He didn't understand the signal and closed the door tighter. The director's wife then ran on stage and offered to double her salary if she finished the play – which she did.

The president of St Bartholomew's Hospital was in the audience and reset her toe behind the scenes later.

FANTASTIC FACTS 1: THE TEN AGES OF SHAKESPEARE

William Shakespeare is the most famous writer in the English language. Yet we don't know a lot about him. Every scrap of paper that mentions him is worth a thousand times its weight in gold.

Someone once said that all we know about Shakespeare could be written on the back of a postcard ... but it would have to be a large postcard with tiny writing! It's not *that* bad!

Shakespeare himself said that life is a bit like a play. We go through it in seven scenes ... or seven *ages*. Shakespeare wrote:

> All the world's a stage,
> And all the men and women merely players:
> They have their exits and their entrances;
> And one man in his time plays many parts,
> His acts being seven ages.[3]

If Shakespeare's life could be divided into seven ages then a diary of his life might look like this...

[3]From Act II Scene VII of the play *As You Like It*, spoken by the character Jaques.

Age 1
At first the infant,
Mewling and puking in the nurse's arms.

26ᵗʰ April

1564. On this day I was christened at Holy Trinity church in Stratford. My father, John Shakespeare, was a glover, wool dealer and money lender. My mother was Mary Arden.

DAD

MUM

Age 2
Then the whining schoolboy, with his satchel,
And shining morning face, creeping like a snail
Unwillingly to school.

My father sends me to school though he struggles to afford it. Business has been poor. He dare not leave the house for fear of being arrested ~~though~~ because of his debts when he goes outside. I wish I could leave this school and work to help my parents. I want to be a poet.

Age 3
And then the lover,
Sighing like a furnace, with a woeful ballad
Made to his mistress' eyebrow.

28th November 1582

Eighteen years old and married with a child on the way. Anne Hathaway is a sweet enough wife. But it is not the poet's life I'd hoped for.

2nd February 1582

Not one child but twins. ANNE Hamnet and Judith! Anne understands. I must leave her and go to London if I am to make a decent living for us all. There is also an accusation of poaching against me. In London I'll be safe.

Age 4
Then a soldier,
Full of strange oaths, and bearded like the pard,
Jealous in honour, sudden and quick in quarrel,
Seeking the bubble reputation
Even in the cannon's mouth.

May 1592

London is a dangerous, squalid, dark and evil place. A man must fight to make his way among the cut-throats, cut-purses, beggars,

and cheats. But my plays are popular.
I will be a success. The plague has
closed the theatres for now. But they'll
reopen. I will write, I'll act .... and
one day I will own shares in my
own company

Age 5

And then the justice,
In fair round belly with good capon lined,
With eyes severe, and beard of formal cut,
Full of wise saws and modern instances;
And so he plays his part.

1597

I have restored my family name in
Stratford. We have a coat of arms from
the crown for our loyal service. I have a
fine house there, New Place, when I
want a break from London.
Sadly, my son Hamnet died last
year, before he could see his
father's success.

Queen Elizabeth admires my
work and with her support we will
build a new theatre in London.
I will be the only
writer and owner of a
theatre, though I'm
growing too old to
act. The world's a
stage and the stage
is a world. So I will
call my theatre
The Globe.

QUEEN
ELIZABETH

THE GLOBE

Age 6
*The sixth age shifts
Into the lean and slipper'd pantaloon,
With spectacles on nose and pouch on side,
His youthful hose well saved, a world too wide
For his shrunk shank; and his big manly voice,
Turning again toward childish treble, pipes
And whistles in his sound.*

<u>1612</u>

The theatre's a life for younger men than me and I do little writing now. I live a settled life in Stratford. I'm a grandfather now, the child is called Elizabeth. I never thought I'd live to see the day when I'd become respectable — a leading local citizen. I entertain the local squires, the men with money and power. But still the visits to my old theatre friends bring me most happiness.

Age 7
*Last scene of all,
That ends this strange eventful history,
Is second childishness and mere oblivion,
Sans* teeth, sans eyes, sans taste, sans everything.*

* "Sans" is French for "without".

1616

My daughters are my comfort and my trouble. Judith married Thomas Quiney, a wild young man — much like young Kit Marlowe.

I think I must protect her when I make my will. And friends say people will be curious about me when I die Even dig me up! So I've composed a verse for my tomb. The last verse that I'll ever write:

JUDITH

QUINEY

> Good friend, for Jesus' sake forbear
> To dig the dust enclosed here.
> Blest be the man that spares these stones,
> And cursed be he that moves my bones.

The rest, as I said in Hamlet, is silence.

Shakespeare died on 23rd April, 1616 … the date that was probably his birthday.

Shakespeare said our lives have *seven* ages … but great artists live on after death. Their work survives, their name survives. Shakespeare has had at least three more ages since his death!

OOH! NASTY!

Age 8

In 1623 Shakespeare's plays were printed in one volume and were performed over and over again. But at first they were not treated with great respect – people began to claim that Will Shakespeare didn't even write them! Delicate audiences didn't like the violence and misery of the tragedies … so they were re-written with happy endings!

Age 9

A hundred and fifty years after his death a great actor, David Garrick, organized a celebration of Shakespeare's work. As Shakespeare's friends had predicted, people were also interested in the man who wrote them. They travelled to Stratford to look over New Place. In 1754 the owner became so fed up with sightseers that he pulled the place down! Now we can't see the home he was so proud of. But the power of the plays survived and Shakespeare lived again through his plays. Shakespeare became a "classic" author. Schools studied him and looked in depth at every word. He never meant this to happen.

Age 10

Now Shakespeare's plays are being enjoyed by modern audiences as they were meant to be – in performance, not in a dusty school-book. But these new performances are often on film rather than on stage. In 1996 there were more scripts by Shakespeare being filmed than by any other single author. As someone wrote in 1996, "Shakespeare is the most popular script-writer in Hollywood." Shakespeare is in his tenth age and where he deserves to be – right at the top.

STORY 2: KING LEAR

King Lear is one of Shakespeare's *tragedies*. A "tragedy" has an unhappy ending in which the hero dies ... and usually lots of other people die at the same time. In *King Lear* they die of everything from a broken neck to a broken heart. Tragic.

The play was written around the year 1605 – one of the most dramatic years in British history, when a group of Catholics plotted to kill the new king, James I. They built up a stock of gunpowder in the cellars of Parliament and waited for the king to arrive. But, the night before James was due to open Parliament, a man was discovered in the cellar. That man was to become more famous than James I! His name was Guy Fawkes.

In that year Shakespeare wrote his play *King Lear*, which shows what happens when a rightful king gives up the throne and divides his kingdom

There are not a lot of laughs in *King Lear*. If you want to entertain your friends and impress your teachers with a performance of this great play then here's a very short version.

Lear today, gone tomorrow

CAST:

King Lear: Ancient British king. Gradually loses his daughters (and his marbles) as the play goes on, till he has none left by the end (daughters or marbles).

Cordelia: Lear's youngest and nicest daughter. Practically a saint and, like a saint, comes to a sticky end.

Goneril: Lear's nasty, evil, cruel, greedy, selfish, jealous and ungrateful daughter. Her only good point is being able to hide any good point.

Regan: Lear's other evil daughter. To have one evil daughter is unlucky, to have two looks like carelessness.

Duke of Gloucester: Ancient British lord. Loses his eyes as the play goes on. Gloucester has one bad child and like Lear, one good child...

Edmund: Gloucester's wicked son. A real trouble-maker. Hates his dad, his brother, King Lear ... but loves the evil Goneril, of course.

Edgar: Gloucester's goody-goody son and a rather goody actor who disguises himself as all sorts of things in order to help the weak and suffering. Creep.[4]

Servant: A servant.

The Fool: Tells the story and tries to keep out of the way of the eye-gouging, stabbing and poisoning, otherwise the play will never end. He's no fool!

---

[4] Not a good part to play. Edgar is one of the few left alive at the end so he doesn't get a good dramatic death scene ... and he probably has the job of burying the others.

Scene 1

The Fool: The scene is ancient Britain and here we are in Lear's windswept castle. It is a dark night ... as nights often are. The great old king is planning to retire and share out his kingdom. When the play starts he is surrounded by his three daughters...

Lear: *Give me the map there. Know that we have divided in three our kingdom ... Tell me, my daughters ... which of you shall we say doth love us most?*

IMPORTANT NOTE: All the characters' words in italics in the following play were written by William Shakespeare.

The Fool: First Goneril stepped forward.

Goneril: *Sir, I love you ... dearer than eyesight ... than life, with grace, health, beauty, honour. As much as a child ever loved.*
(Lear rips off one third of the map and gives it to her.)

Lear: What a wonderful daughter. Obviously takes after her father! We make thee queen of all the land from this line to this.

Goneril: Thanks, dad-your-highness. You'll not regret this ... (aside) much!

Lear: Our dearest Regan ... speak!

Regan: *I am made of that self metal as my sister.*

Lear: What a lovely girl! I've made a right good job of bringing up these two. *To thee and thine hereditary ever remain this ample third of our fair kingdom.*

Regan: Thanks, dad-your-highness. A generous, loving parent ... (aside) and a right mug if you ask me!

The Fool: But little Cordelia loved him more than words can say! So when he turned to her and said...

Lear: *Speak!*
The Fool: She said...
Cordelia: *Nothing, my lord.*
Lear: *Nothing!*
Cordelia: *Nothing.*

Lear: *Nothing will come of nothing. Speak again.*

Cordelia: *I cannot heave my heart into my mouth.*

The Fool: This meant she couldn't speak her heart – not that she couldn't vomit. Anyway, the king was furious...

Lear: *Hence, and avoid my sight!* Obviously YOU take after your mother, not me. She didn't know which side her bread was buttered on either.

Cordelia: Cordelia leaves you.

(Cordelia leaves as the king rips her part of the map in two and gives a piece each to Goneril and Regan. They grasp it greedily and follow. Lear leaves shaking his head.)

The Fool: Lear had given his kingdom away. But if he expected Goneril and Regan to look after him, he had another thing coming...

Scene 2

The Fool: First the old king went to stay with Goneril. She soon grew tired of him and his followers.

Goneril: Look here, dad-your-ex-highness. *Here do you keep a hundred knights and squires, men so disordered ... that this our court is like a riotous inn ... more like a tavern than a palace. You strike my people!*

Lear: *Darkness and devils! Saddle my horses; call my train together. I'll not trouble thee ... Detested kite!* How about giving me my land back?

Goneril: No chance, you senile goat.

Lear: *Let it be so: I have another daughter.* I'll bet she's not such a rotten little ratbag!

The Fool: And so he stomped off in a huff to stay with daughter Regan...

Lear: *Good morrow to you.*

Regan: *I am glad to see your highness.*

Lear: *Regan, I think you are.*

Regan: The only problem is, dad-your-ex-highness, I don't have a lot of room in my castles for you and your knights. So, I've had a great idea. *Return you to my sister.*

Lear: *Return to her? ... Never, Regan ... Daughter, do not make me mad. I will not trouble thee, my child; farewell.*

(He stomps off and she calls after him ...)

Regan: Please yourself. I never could stand ranting wrinklies!

The Fool: As a storm broke, the old king went into the wild night. Ahhhh!

Regan: Shut up the doors, it is a wild night.

Servant: It's a bit wet and windy for the old bloke, your highness.

Regan: Tough.

Servant: Have you no heart?

Regan: Yes ... but I keep it in the freezer.

(She leaves the stage. The servant follows, muttering.)

Servant: Cor! Regan's not half ruthless.

The Fool: But old King Lear was roof-less. He wandered onto the moors, moaning...

Scene 3

Lear: Moan! Moan! Moan! Oh, moaney, moaney, moaney! *Such a night to shut me out! ... O Regan, Goneril! Your old kind father.*

The Fool: And there he met Edgar, son of the Duke of Gloucester, disguised as a madman. The disguise was so his evil brother Edmund couldn't find him and kill him.

Edgar: *Pillicock sat on Pillicock-hill: Halloo, halloo, loo, loo! ... Tom's a-cold ... Poor Tom; that eats the swimming frog, the toad, the tadpole, eats cow-dung ... swallows the old rat and the ditch-dog ... Fie, foh, and fum, I smell the blood of a British man.[5]*

The Fool: It was a very good act! Then the Duke of Gloucester arrived. He didn't recognize his son, Edgar, but he did offer to rescue the king...

[5] Yes, I know it's hard to believe but Will Shakespeare really did write those lines too.

Gloucester: Hoy! You over there! Yes, you with the bowl of porridge for a brain. *Where is the king, my master?*

Edgar: Here, sir.

(He points to Lear on the ground.)

Gloucester: *Take up thy master and follow me.*

(As Edgar picks up Lear in a fireman's lift he turns to the audience.)

Edgar: That's a nice way to talk to someone – even someone pretending to be a porridge-brain! If he wasn't me dad I'd probably smack him in the mouth.

Scene 4

The Fool: When the two sisters heard that Gloucester had rescued their dad they were mad!

Regan: *Hang him instantly!*

Goneril: *Pluck out his eyes!*

The Fool: Evil Cornwall, Regan's husband, brought the duke before the sisters...

Regan: *O, filthy traitor!*

Gloucester: *I'm none!*

Cornwall: *Upon these eyes of thine I'll set my foot.*

The Fool: And he stuck his spur into Gloucester's eye. But a brave servant stepped forward.

Gloucester: Ouch! Me eye! Here ... what's today's date?

The Fool: 22nd November, why?

Gloucester: Cos I've always wanted a blind date.

The Fool: With jokes like that he deserved to lose his tongue as well. But the kindly servant stepped forward.

Servant: *Hold your hand, my lord!* I can't see the point of this.

Cornwall: Gloucester won't see the point of anything when I've ripped out his other eye! So push off, you interfering toe-rag.

(They fight. Cornwall is wounded. Regan takes a sword and stabs the servant.)

Servant: *O! I am slain! ... O!*

(Wounded servant staggers off to die.)

The Fool: The wounded Cornwall turned back to Gloucester...

Gloucester: *Oh you gods!*

Cornwall: *Out, vile jelly!*

The Fool: And he plucked out the other eye!

Regan: *Go thrust him out at gates!*

(Gloucester is thrown out by Cornwall. Regan and Goneril follow them off stage.)

The Fool: Gloucester staggered out where he met his good son Edgar and King Lear. There were lots of hugs and kisses. The three went off to meet Cordelia who was leading an army to beat her evil sisters. There were more hugs and kisses.

Lear: *I think this lady to be my child, Cordelia!*

Cordelia: *And so I am! I am!*

The Fool: But before you think this is going to be a happy ending, you have to remember blind Gloucester had another son. The wicked Edmund who had taken sides with Goneril and Regan . . .

Scene 5

The Fool: Lear's army fought wicked Edmund's and . . .

Edgar: *King Lear hath lost! He and his daughter taken!*

(Edgar rushes off. Evil Edmund enters with Lear and Cordelia; they are his prisoners.)

Edmund: *Some officers, take them away!*

Lear: *Come, let's away to prison. We two alone will sing like birds in the cage.*

Cordelia: I don't know the words of *Like Birds in the Cage*.

Lear: You just take your socks off and hum.

Edmund: *Take them away!*

(Lear and Cordelia go to prison. Regan staggers on.)

The Fool: Meanwhile, Goneril has poisoned Regan...

Regan: *I am not well ... Sick! O, sick ... My sickness grows upon me.*

The Fool: But before she dies she stabs sister Goneril!

(Goneril and Regan stagger off to die.)

Goneril: That wasn't a very sisterly thing to do!

Regan: It wasn't very nice poisoning me!

Goneril: I never liked you. Ever since you pinched my rattle when we were kids.

Regan: I also dipped your dummy in my potty.

Goneril: Yeuch! You never told me that. You could have poisoned me.

Regan: I just did, sis. I just did!

The Fool: Three gone if you include Regan's husband, Cornwall the eye-gouger, who died of the servant's wound – but still a few more corpses to go before the end.

(Edgar enters and confronts Edmund.)

Edgar: *Draw thy sword!*

Edmund: *I should ask thy name!*

(They fight. Edmund falls, wounded.)

Edgar: *My name is Edgar and thy father's son.*

Edmund: I had a brother called Edgar!

Edgar: That's me, sunshine.

Edmund: That wasn't a very brotherly thing to do!

Edgar: I never liked you. You never let me play with your train set.

(Edmund staggers off to die.)

The Fool: Another two gone – Gloucester has died of a broken heart and now Edmund's been stabbed. Hope you're counting. Here's another one...

(Lear enters, carrying dead Cordelia.)

Lear: *Howl! Howl! Howl! ... She's gone forever.*

The Fool: He's right. He's not as mad as he was! Cordelia was hanged by a prison guard.

Lear: She was always a highly strung girl. *I killed the slave that was hanging thee!*

The Fool: That's another one if you're counting.

(Lear falls.)

Edgar: *He faints! My lord, My lord!*

(Checks Lear's pulse)

He is gone.

The Fool: So Lear died of a broken heart too. And that only left Edgar ... and me, of course ... and I don't feel too grand myself. Everyone else is dead, so Edgar becomes king.

(Edgar picks up Lear's crown and puts it on. He then drags the corpse off stage while the Fool grabs Cordelia's body by the ankles and follows.)

The Fool: Now that's what I call a tragedy. The tragedy known as...

(Cordelia looks up from the floor.)

Cordelia: Happy Families!

The Fool: The end!

Did you know...?
In Stratford in the 1980s a theatre company performed *King Lear* with lots of realistic violence. For the scene in which Gloucester has his eyes torn out, the stage manager had made eyes out of a jelly substance; the actors pretended to tear them from the victim's eye sockets and throw them away.

On the first night the scene went beautifully – the audience gasped with horror. But on the second night the actors could hardly act. They were choking, trying to say the sad words yet bursting to laugh instead. Why? Because the jelly eyes had stuck to the scenery. The actors were trying to act seriously with a pair of jelly eyes staring at them!

FANTASTIC FACTS 2: SHAKESPEARE'S THEATRE

When Will Shakespeare arrived in London in 1587 he arrived at an exciting time. Most entertainments were cruel "sports" like bear-baiting and cock-fighting. Between the "sports" simple plays were performed – knockabout comedies with silly stories. But at that time serious plays were being written and performed and were becoming popular.

Theatre companies usually had about eight men, and a few boys who were trained to play the women's parts. The theatre companies would buy plays from writers, buy costumes from tailors and put on the plays. They would share costs and share the money the public paid to see them. These men were called, not surprisingly, "sharers".

The sharers hired extra actors when plays needed them, and these extras were called, not surprisingly, "hirelings". Shakespeare probably learned about the theatre by becoming a hireling, then trying his hand at writing for a company. Being quite a sharp businessman he soon became a sharer and helped to build for his company a new theatre, *The Globe*.

The theatres were large open-air circles of seats with a stage at one side.

If you are reading Shakespeare's plays, then it helps to know a little about the theatre world in which they were performed. Try this quick quiz and discover some curious facts and learn how menacing Shakespeare's world of theatre could be...

TEN BEST DANGEROUSLY DRAMATIC FACTS!

1 Most of the audience stood on the ground around the stage to watch the play. These "groundlings" only paid a penny. Where were the best seats for important spectators?

    A In a small room (called a "box") with a window onto the stage.

    B In an armchair in front of the stage.

    C On the stage itself.

2 Stage managers had the job of making sound effects for storms or battles. But when it came to making a sound effect of a cannon, they just fired a cannon – stuffed with paper, not a cannon-ball! When this happened in 1613 something went wrong. What was it?

    A The paper used to stuff the cannon was the script; it blew away and no one knew their lines.

B The burning paper was blown onto the thatched roof of the theatre, where it started a fire that burned the theatre down.

C The noise shocked two old women in the audience so much that they both died of a heart attack.

3 Cannon-balls weren't used in stage cannons, but pistols used real bullets at one time. In 1587, during a play by Christopher Marlowe, one actor had to shoot another. He aimed to *miss* of course. What went wrong?

A He hit the other actor.

B He missed the actor but killed a woman in the audience.

C He missed the other actor but killed a bird which fell onto the stage and injured the actor with the pistol.

4 The Church was against play performances in the city of London. They said that plays were sinful and kept people from going to church. What else were plays blamed for?

A The plague.

B Drunkenness.

C Starving children.

5 When London theatres closed in 1592 and 1593 the actors went on tour around the country. This caused them special problems. What were they?

A They couldn't find theatres to perform in.
B They kept getting lost because there were no good maps.

C They couldn't make enough money to eat.

6 Rich people could "buy" a performance of a play. The company would come to their house (or palace or castle), set up in a hall and give a private performance for friends of the owner. A man called Gamaliel Ratsey paid a company to perform for him at his country house. What happened next?

A The actors were robbed by a highwayman and lost their 40 shillings.
B Gamaliel Ratsey refused to hand over the money and threw them out because their play was not good enough.
C Gamaliel Ratsey enjoyed the play so much he built the company a theatre so they would always have a home.

7 Playwrights struggled to make a living. They were paid a few shillings for a play then didn't get another penny, even if the play was a great success and the theatre managers made a fortune. So playwrights took other jobs to make some money. Christopher Marlowe, who was writing when Shakespeare arrived in London had a curious job. What was it?

A He caught rats for the rat-pit at the theatre where dogs fought and killed them.

B He made costumes for the actors in his plays and was famous for his glittering royal robes.

C He was a spy, working for Elizabeth I's government to seek out Catholic traitors.

8 Shakespeare shared his theatres with some cruel sports but occasionally made use of them to add interest to his plays. What did he add to his play *The Winter's Tale*?

A A cock fight where two characters bet on the result.

B A character chased off the stage by a bear.

C A dancing monkey.

9 Writing plays could be a dangerous business. Ben Jonson spent time in jail for writing a play that insulted King James. Shakespeare wrote plays that supported the king or queen but even he ended in very deep trouble. How?

   A He wrote a play that insulted Henry VIII and Henry was Elizabeth I's father. She was furious.

   B He wrote a play that praised Catholics at a time when James I had almost been blown up by a Catholic plot that involved Guy Fawkes.

   C He performed his play *Richard II* which showed a monarch being overthrown. He performed it for a group who were plotting to overthrow Elizabeth at that time.

10 Theatre companies were always having trouble with theatre buildings. They were closed by the law or the owners wanted too much money for plays to be performed. Shakespeare and his friends came up with a daring plan when their "Theatre" building was closed down. What was it?

   A They knocked the building down and carried it to a new piece of land that they owned.

B They showed plays anyway and refused to stop when the magistrates ordered them to.

C They performed in front of Elizabeth I's palace as a protest and got the support of the queen to re-open the theatre.

Answers:

1-C The most important people sat on stools on the stage. The groundlings enjoyed watching the famous guests as much as they did the plays at times! There is a story about one of Shakespeare's greatest fans, Queen Elizabeth I. She not only sat on the stage but wandered across it and waved to the audience while the actors were trying to perform! One day Will Shakespeare himself was playing a part when the queen wandered across to say "Hello".

He carried on acting and ignored her. So she dropped a glove. Shakespeare picked up the glove, added a couple of extra lines to explain the glove in the play, then left the stage. Elizabeth thought this was hilarious! It didn't always end so happily. At one performance a spectator argued with someone blocking his view by sitting on the stage – one drew his sword and killed the other.

2 -B The thatch caught fire but without a great amount of smoke and flame. The audience thought someone would deal with it and carried on watching the play. When they realized that the whole place was on fire they left in a hurry. No one was hurt except one man whose trousers caught fire. A kind friend poured a bottle of beer over him to put out the flames. The theatre was totally rebuilt ... with *tiles* on the roof!

3-B The accidental death of a member of an audience caused a great deal of trouble for theatres in 1587, the year that Shakespeare arrived in London to make his living as a playwright. Some people were really keen to close down all theatres and such accidents gave them an excuse. Local councils objected to plays then in the same way some councils object to large pop concerts now. They said that the streets were blocked by crowds of spectators, there were lots of fights among the audiences and villains took advantage of the crowding to commit their crimes.

4-A Theatres were closed in 1592 because there was an outbreak of plague in London. People crowding together in a theatre could spread the plague – so closing the theatres made sense. But some priests said theatres *caused* the plague. One argued, "Sin causes the plague and plays cause sin. So plays cause the plague."

5-C Theatre companies didn't need theatres to perform in. They could set up a platform in the yard of an inn and give their performance. But travelling around, feeding horses and staying at inns cost money, and the money came out of the actors' wages. They earned half what they would have been paid in London. Some companies became so desperate they sold their playscripts and their costumes so they'd have enough money for food.

6-A The actors headed home next day but were robbed

by a highwayman who said, "I want the 40 shillings Gamaliel Ratsey paid you last night". How did the highwayman know about Gamaliel Ratsey's 40 shillings? Because under the mask it *was* Gamaliel Ratsey! The actors survived the frightening experience ... but Gamaliel Ratsey didn't for very long. He was caught and hanged for his thieving ways.

7-C Marlowe was a spy. He was killed in a fight in an eating house in London. It was made to look like an accident, but most historians now believe he was murdered because of his spying activities. Another playwright of the time, Ben Jonson, was involved in the spying that led to Guy Fawkes being arrested. Shakespeare was more careful – he made extra money by becoming a theatre "sharer" but some modern writers believe that even he could have been caught up in the Elizabethan spy game.

8-B The bear was a tame one! But the character had to face a terrible danger in a strange land – Shakespeare decided there was nothing more dangerous than a bear, so he borrowed one for the performances. The audiences must have loved it! Modern stage managers have a bit more trouble finding ways of having the character chased off the stage. An actor in a bear costume just doesn't look as good.

9-C The Earl of Essex gathered a group of rebels together and plotted to replace Elizabeth on the throne of England. They hired Shakespeare to perform the play *Richard II* about a similar rebellion because it amused them. Shakespeare probably did not realize what was going on; still, he was lucky not to be executed when the angry Elizabeth found out. Almost two hundred years after Shakespeare's death *King Lear* was banned because it showed a mad king – at a time when the British king George III was mad.

10-A Shakespeare hired carpenters and labourers to cut down the old theatre and carry it, plank by plank, across the river to a new site. There it was re-built and given a new name – *The Globe*. The site of *The Globe* was uncovered by archaeologists in the 1980s and rebuilt as a modern replica in the 1990s. The new *Globe* is a great achievement … but to move the original *Globe* across the River Thames, was an amazing and daring idea. Perhaps only a man like Shakespeare could have planned that!

STORY 3: TWELFTH NIGHT

Twelfth Night, another comedy, was written around 1601. Elizabeth was growing old and her favourite, the Earl of Essex, led a rebellion to grab the throne for himself. He called for the people of England to support him … the people of England said, "No, thank you!" and Essex looked a little silly.

Essex said, "Sorry," to Elizabeth.

Elizabeth said, "You will be." He went to the block, the axe went on his neck … and his head went on the grass.

Nearly as entertaining as a Shakespeare play!

Shakespeare's plays had very little scenery and no lighting – the plays were usually set up in the open air and performed in daylight. Yet this didn't stop him from writing exciting and spectacular scenes. In *The Tempest*, for example, the play opens with a ship-wreck and in *Twelfth Night* survivors of a storm appear on a rocky beach! The stage helpers would be thumping sheets of metal backstage to create the sounds of a storm while the actors would be rushing around, shouting and panicking as if their ship was going down. The water, the ship and the storm were all in Shakespeare's words and in the imaginations of the audience.

Shakespeare's stage was practically empty. It was *nowhere* … so it could quickly become *anywhere*!

Twelfth Night is a comedy, but a very cruel one. The main joke involves driving a pompous (but pathetic) man insane. Not funny at all.

MALVOLIO'S MADNESS

1 Sebastian and Viola sailed across a stormy sea;
They reached Illyria's coast, the ship went down.
The brother and the sister lost each other in the waves;
Each lived … each thought the other one had drowned!

Oh, my poor brother.[6]

[6]All the words in italics are written by Shakespeare.

2 Viola landed safely and she found some new, dry clothes;
But clothes that made her look just like a boy.
She went off to the palace of Illyria's Count Orsino,
A lovesick man whose life had seen no joy.

I can sing, and speak to him in many sorts of music.

3 He loved the fair Olivia, but she'd no love in return.
She wouldn't even read Orsino's letters.
And so he sent Viola with his messages of love,
And hoped that her smooth talk would do much better.

Stand at her doors ... till those have audience.

I'll do my best

4 But at Olivia's house her uncle, fat Sir Toby Belch,
Had plans to wed Olivia to his friend…
A limp and feeble straw-haired knight, Sir Andrew
Aguecheek…
And they plotted how to gain their wicked ends.

5 Now, when the young Viola turned up at Olivia's gate
Malvolio, the butler, barred her way.
Viola got her message through, Olivia was impressed,
And liked Viola more than words can say.

6 Malvolio was angry and he came across Sir Toby
With Sir Andrew Aguecheek in drunken song.
He threatened that he'd have Olivia throw the drunkards
out.
So Sir Toby planned revenge both cruel and wrong.

7 Maria was a serving maid, and friend of fat Sir Toby,
Whose writing was quite like Olivia's style.
She'd write a loving letter for Malvolio to find,
Saying how she longed to see the butler smile.

8 The letter said Olivia wanted him in yellow stockings,
(In truth a colour that the lady hated.)
They dropped the letter on the path. Malvolio picked it up.
He read it while the plotters smiled ... and waited.

9 So when the butler turned up at his mistress' room next day,
In those stockings, yellow and quite vile,
He said he knew Olivia loved him ... said he loved her too;
A crazy grin on his face all the while!

10 Olivia was frightened and was sure the man was mad,
She called Sir Toby Belch to save her, please!
She ordered that the butler should be locked in some dark cell,
Until the fit of madness had been eased.

11 Olivia sent to see Viola, said that she would listen
If Viola brought a message from the Count.
Sir Toby feared his plans to wed his niece to Aguecheek
Would fail. He had to drive Viola out!

12 Sir Toby told Sir Andrew that he'd have to fight Viola;
Then he told Viola just the same.
The fighters were quite terrified for both thought they would die;
Sir Toby laughed as he enjoyed the game.

13 The Captain of the storm-wrecked ship rushed in and stepped between
As they flapped with feeble swords at one another.
He thought that he had come to save Sebastian from the fight,
For Viola looked exactly like her brother.

14 Sebastian? Viola thought! That means he's still alive!
Her long lost brother and her closest friend.
The brother he was married to Olivia that same day,
And so his story reached a happy end.

15 Viola, as a woman, now could love the Duke Orsino
They too planned to marry in a while.
Sir Toby weds Maria; only Andrew Aguecheek
Was left to wander witless and alone.

16 Malvolio at last was freed from his dark prison cell.
He showed the letter ... proved that he was sane.
His pride and life were broken by Sir Toby's foolish game.
And his life would never be the same again.

> *I'll be revenged on the whole pack of you.*

Did you know...?
Twelfth Night is not about a twelfth night of anything!
The twelfth night *after* Christmas is the end of the
Christmas period (January 6th) when we take down
our decorations. In Shakespeare's day it was the night
when people could relax again after the religious
celebrations and enjoy a play. He wrote this play to
be performed on a twelfth night in the reign of
Elizabeth I.

FANTASTIC FACTS 3: TEN BEST ACTORS' TALES

William Shakespeare was very lucky that he arrived in London when he did. For at that time there were some clever and experienced actors working in the theatre. Actors like Edward Alleyn were stars – and young Shakespeare could try out speeches with the great man and get advice on how to make them work on stage.

Edward Alleyn could be very fussy. One of his scripts has survived and he has scribbled notes complaining about how long and boring the speech is. But that was a Robert Greene play, not a Shakespeare play!

Here are the ten best stories about great Shakespearean actors...

STAGE FRIGHTS

1 **Will Kemp.** Kemp was one of the most popular members of Shakespeare's theatre company. He was as much a clown and a dancer as an actor. Modern performers often do things to get their names in the papers – publicity stunts. Kemp knew all about publicity stunts four hundred years ago. In 1599 he left the theatre company to *dance* from London to

Norwich. This was such a success that he then danced over the Alps into Italy. Actors don't make that sort of effort to get noticed nowadays!

2 David Garrick 1717 – 1791. In 1769 Garrick produced the plays in Stratford-upon-Avon to celebrate the 200th anniversary of Shakespeare's birth (although *you* will have spotted it was in fact Shakespeare's 205th birthday!) This was really the start of a new popular interest in Shakespeare's plays. But the "popular" audience caused problems. One night Garrick was playing King Lear and

reached the scene where he wept over his dead daughter Cordelia. Garrick looked up at the audience and almost choked. He had to run off stage. Other actors followed and finally "dead" Cordelia opened her eyes and followed them in hysterical laughter. What had the actors seen? A butcher sitting in the front row with his dog. The butcher had become too hot, so he'd taken off his powdered wig and stuck it on the dog's head. The sight made Garrick and his actors laugh too much to go on with the performance. Perhaps the dog was hoping for a part in *The Winter's Tail!*

3 John Philip Kemble 1757 – 1823. Famous for his dramatic acting style with long silences in the middle of speeches. During a performance of Shakespeare's *Coriolanus* an apple landed on the stage. Kemble could have ignored it and carried on. Instead he picked it up, walked to the front of the stage and demanded to know who had thrown it. "I offer one hundred guineas to the person who will tell me the name of the ruffian who

threw this object!" A voice from the gallery called back that it was a slightly drunken woman who'd thrown it, but she wasn't aiming at the stage and she was very sorry. Kemble asked her friends to keep her in order, then he coolly finished the performance. Maybe she thought she was watching *Core-iolanus!*

4 Sarah Kemble Siddons 1755 – 1831. Sister to John Philip Kemble and with the same passionate style. Sarah Siddons was extremely popular in Shakespeare plays but the audience could become carried away and call out

advice. In *Romeo and Juliet* she was about to drink the cup of poison when someone called out, "That's right lass – sup it up!" Her most famous performance was as Lady Macbeth. When she played it for the last time the audience cheered non-stop after she left the stage. There was still a quarter of an hour of the play to go but the audience wouldn't stop cheering her. In the end the actors gave up and that performance was never finished.

5 Edmund Kean 1787 – 1833. Kean began acting at the age of four and became the most popular actor of his time. He was a small man but with a powerful voice and hypnotic eyes. He was also very fond of alcohol. One night he became too drunk to play Shylock in *The Merchant of Venice* so his friends came up with an excuse for him. They said he was travelling to the theatre when a flock

of geese frightened his horses, his coach overturned and he dislocated his shoulder. The trouble was that he was stuck with the story. He had to make his face pale with make-up when people called to see him. Then he returned to the stage to play *Macbeth* and *Othello* just a few days after his "accident". So he played the parts with his arm in a sling! The audiences were amazed at his courage ... and no one ever discovered he was a cheat.

6 William Charles Macready 1793 – 1873. This English actor experienced as much trouble with *King Lear* as Garrick had a hundred years before him. The stage manager was given a list of the items that the actors would need on stage. But unfortunately he was a very poor reader and made an hilarious mistake. When King Lear divides up his kingdom the character needs a map. Macready called for the map . . . but

it wasn't there. Instead an actor marched on stage with a MOP! Macready grabbed the man by the scruff of the neck and threw him (and the mop) off stage. The audience enjoyed it; after all, there are not a lot of laughs in *Lear*.

7 Barry Sullivan 1821 – 1891. Barry Sullivan had been an actor in popular plays and one of his best-known roles was as Sailor William. His hornpipe dance always brought the house down. He then tried playing more serious parts and was given the lead part in

Shakespeare's *Hamlet*. Unfortunately, one of his audiences was full of drunken sailors. "Dance the hornpipe, Barry!" they yelled as he was trying to do a dramatic scene. He carried on playing Hamlet. "Dance the hornpipe or I'll come down there and make you!" a sailor threatened. Barry danced the hornpipe. The audience cheered wildly ... then the actor went back to playing Hamlet and the audience watched happily.

8 Robert Mantell 1854 – 1928. On one occasion Mantell had the bad luck to be playing Shakespeare's *Richard III* with a really terrible crew of stage workers. The curtains were drawn across the front of the stage and Mantell was acting in front of them. Behind the curtains the stage workers were clattering round and making a dreadful noise. Then one of the stage hands pushed through the  curtain shoving Mantell in the back. The actor was almost catapulted into the audience. The next time he was making a speech in front of the curtains the same thing happened ... but this time Mantell was ready for it. He took the character's dagger – a real one – and stabbed the curtain with it. There was a howl of pain and Mantell was able to complete the scene in peace.

When he came off stage he discovered he'd stabbed a stage hand in the leg. He then threatened to do the same to the others if they made another mistake. They didn't! As Shakespeare might have said, "All's well that ends well".

9 Sir Herbert Beerbohm Tree 1853 – 1917. In one production Tree not only played the part of Hamlet but also directed the play. He arranged for a group of singers to sing like a choir of angels when he, Hamlet, died. It all went well until one night the musical director was missing and the "angels" had to sing without him to lead them. Hamlet died and the angels sang … totally out of tune. They sounded like wailing cats. In the end Tree couldn't

stand any more. Hamlet's dead body stood up and cried, "Oh, those bloody angels!" and charged furiously off stage. The angels very wisely ran and locked themselves in their dressing room till Tree had gone. (The angels must have prayed Tree would leaf them alone.)

10 Sir Laurence Olivier 1907 – 1989. Olivier was one of the twentieth century's greatest Shakespearean actors. He claimed that acting Shakespeare was a really dangerous job. There were all of those sword fights for a start. In a 1935 production of *Romeo and Juliet* he cut an actor's hand so badly that his thumb was hanging by a thread. Olivier himself suffered a slashed chest from a sword. Apart from broken bones and torn muscles two of his worst accidents happened off stage. Filming a Shakespeare play should have been safe, but as Olivier looked through

the viewfinder of a movie camera a galloping horse charged into the camera and smashed his face. After a performance of *Hamlet* Olivier was wearing a sword and backing away from a reporter who wanted to interview him. The sword became wedged in a lighting switchboard and Olivier was almost electrocuted. Nearly a shocking end to a great career.

STORY 4: THE TEMPEST

By the year 1611 William Shakespeare was writing his last play – *The Tempest*. In the next five years before his death he probably helped write another two, but most Shakespeare experts agree that *The Tempest* was his last complete one. Why did he retire to his home in Stratford when he was just 47 years old? Was he worn out, or ill, or just so rich he wanted an easy life? Or was London with its constant plagues too dangerous?

You can be pretty sure he didn't simply run out of ideas. Shakespeare read many history books for ideas and he read travel stories from all round the world. In 1610, for example, he would have read the reports of Sir George Somers' shipwreck in Bermuda and may even have spoken to some survivors. So he wrote his great "shipwreck" play, *The Tempest*.

He took the idea of a storm driving a ship onto an island and asked himself,

> *What would happen if the storm wasn't natural and the shipwreck wasn't an accident? What if the storm was deliberately whipped up by a magician because he wanted the travellers on his island?*

And, when it came to performing the part of the magician, who should play the part? William Shakespeare himself, of course! Possibly the last great part he played.

Like *A Midsummer Night's Dream*, this play is a "dream" play – the characters "live" for a while upon the stage and then vanish.

If Shakespeare did play the part of Prospero, the magician, then he said farewell to his audiences with a speech that summed up the world of theatre:

> *These our actors ... were all spirits and*
> *Are melted into air, into thin air...*
> *We are such stuff*
> *As dreams are made on; and our little life*
> *Is rounded with a sleep.*

Prospero's daughter was named Miranda. Her view of the strange events would be an interesting one. Suppose she had written a diary…

MIRANDA'S DIARY

Dear Diary,

Date: The summer of my fifteenth year.

I wonder what a MAN looks like? All I can remember is living on this island with my father, Prospero. Yes I KNOW he's a man, but he's OLD.

We came to the island when I was a child — just three years old. And now, **DADDY** father says, I am about fifteen. He taught me to read, to write and how to know the plants on the island — the ones that will heal 🌸 and the ones that will harm. 🌿 Father has often promised to tell me how we came to be here but he stopped before he finished the story.

Today he handed me this book. He told me it is what's called a "diary". He says that I'm to keep a record of what happens, for I'll see wonders in the next few days the like of which I'll never see again! But he will tell me nothing more. What can I write? I can tell you a little about the island.

Of course there were creatures on it when we landed. The greatest and clumsiest was Caliban. Father told me that Caliban was the son of a witch called Sycorax who owned the island before she died.

CALIBAN

He treated poor Caliban well, until one day Caliban attacked me. For that crime father turned him into a slave. My father has a magic of his own, even stronger than Sycorax's and he says that Caliban is in his power. But I sometimes catch Caliban watching me with a look of evil on his face. I know he's planning his revenge. What if father's power fails? Or if he dies? Why won't he teach me his magic?

Perhaps Ariel will protect me. Ariel is a spirit who takes many forms and sometimes he's invisible. He refused to help Sycorax so she locked him inside a

ARIEL

87

pine tree and father used his magic to release him. Ariel is grateful to father for this, but sometimes I think he too could turn evil without father's magic to control him.

Day 2:

Oh what a strange, exciting and frightening day!

I woke to the sound of thunder and thought at first it was a summer storm. I wandered up to the cliff tops — I knew Ariel would protect me from lightning.

I looked out to sea and felt the wind trying to blow me over the edge of the cliff. Yet there, in the sea was a huge wooden ship with shredded sails being driven towards the cliffs. No wind blows both ways at the same time. I knew it was magical and I knew my father had stirred up the elements to drive the ship ashore.

People on the decks were being thrown into the water by waves that looked like giant hands and swept towards the rocky shore. Those poor souls! I wept and ran back to my father's cell where he sat calmly, his huge cloak wrapped around him.

"Save them!" I cried.

"There's no harm," he said in a voice so soft it was almost swallowed by the screeching wind. "No one will be hurt."

"But why have you done this?"

"I did it for you," he said.

"I don't understand," I moaned.

He took off his cloak of magic and held my hand.

"I've often tried to tell you the truth about our existance here," he said. "Now it is time I did so."

My father stirred the flickering twigs of the fire into a sparkling blaze. "I am the Duke of Milan. Twelve years ago I spent my time studying the magical arts and left my brother Antonio to govern the country. The treacherous man united with Alonso, King of Naples to overthrow me. One night they took us from our palace and cast us adrift in a boat."

"Why didn't they simply kill us?" I asked.

"The people loved me too much. They didn't want our blood on their ANTONIO hands. But the ship they put us in was so rotten even the rats had left. It was as good as

ANTONIO

ALONSO

89

murder." Somehow, he explained, we had survived and were washed up on the shore of this island. His face was as dark as the storm-struck sea. I had seen him this way before when he heard of Caliban's attack on me. He had avenged himself on Caliban. Now he was seeking vengeance on the poor people in that ship.

"Who are they?" I asked. "Who are the people on that ship?"

"My enemies," he replied simply, and his mouth set hard as the rocks on the shore.

"Alonso and Antonio?" I asked.

He waved a hand, impatient at my questions. "You are sleepy," he said. "You cannot help yourself. You have to go to sleep."

And so I sank into a deep and dreamless sleep.

When I awoke it was as if the storm was nothing but a dream.

Day 3:

And when I awoke I thought I saw a spirit. Ariel brought the thing in from the shore, wet and exhausted. It was the most beautiful thing I have ever seen.

It spoke. It was a MAN! A young man called Ferdinand. It seems he was the son of my father's greatest enemy, King Alonso. My father turned on the young man furiously. "You're a spy!" he ranted.

FERDINAND

"I'm no spy," bewildered Ferdinand replied and I believed him.

"Nothing evil could live in a body as lovely as that!" I tried to argue.

My father silenced me angrily. He ordered me not to speak to the young man. "You think Caliban is ugly? Men would think Ferdinand is uglier!" He snorted.

My father enslaved the young man. I tried to tell Ferdinand that Prospero was not usually so cruel but he was led away in chains to work for us.

Day 4:
Just when it seemed that things could grow no stranger ....they did! I watched Ferdinand as he was forced to move thousands of logs and pile them up. He worked without complaining.

I offered to help but he would not let me. He told me I was beautiful........... something I never knew. And then he told me that he loved me. I knew nothing about love but I believed that's what I felt too. I was so happy that I cried and could not understand why happiness can make you weep.

Then my father arrived with news that Ferdinand's father and the evil Antonio were alive. Father had planned to destroy them all in revenge, but Ferdinand proved such a good man that instead father decided two things.

First he would allow Antonio to live if he gave back the Dukedom of Milan.

And secondly, and most wondrously .... he would approve if Ferdinand wanted to marry me!

It seems the enslaving of Ferdinand was father's test to see if the young man was fit to be my husband. Ferdinand had passed the test.

Tomorrow we sail from this island for Italy.

Day 5:

Prospero, my father, has given up his magic. His books have been dropped in the deepest part of the ocean. He will spend the rest of his life trying to be a good duke to the loyal people of Milan.

Father has no magic to control the weather now; so the fair winds that are blowing us across the sea to Italy are probably the farewell gift of the spirit Ariel. Father freed him before we left.

Sad Caliban is left alone, the ruler of his kingdom but with no people left to rule.

Two days ago I had seen no man but my father and the savage Caliban. Now there are sailors and the king with all his nobles. "Oh brave new world that has such people in it."

Did you know...?

Shakespeare read travel books about people from other countries; when he wanted a villain he took the word Cannibal, changed the letters around and came up with the name "Caliban" – the monstrous and savage inhabitant of the island in *The Tempest*.

FANTASTIC FACTS 4 – THE SHAKESPEARE TIMELINE

Shakespeare lived through exciting times. The simple, superstitious days of the Middle Ages were giving way to the modern age.

The Tudors were on the throne during his early life and London was one of the greatest and most lively cities in the world.

Shakespeare did not set his plays in England in the time of Elizabeth I or James I. But the world of the playwright had a powerful influence on his writing. To understand Shakespeare we really need to understand his world. Which of these ten events happened during Shakespeare's lifetime and which affected his writing?

QUICK QUIZ

During Shakespeare's lifetime:

1 Christopher Columbus discovered America – Yes/No?

2 The Spanish Armada tried to invade England – Yes/No?

3 The Black Death killed half the population of Europe – Yes/No?

4 Guy Fawkes tried to blow up Parliament – Yes/No?

5 Witches were burned at the stake – Yes/No?

6 Mary Queen of Scots was executed – Yes/No?

7 The printing press was invented – Yes/No?

8 The government set up a team of international spies – Yes/No?

9 The Spanish were accused of trying to assassinate Elizabeth I – Yes/No?

10 English settlers in America were saved by a young Native American girl called Pocahontas – Yes/No?

How did you do?

1 No. Christopher Columbus discovered America in 1492, a hundred years before Shakespeare was writing. BUT the Elizabethans were still thrilled by the mystery and adventure of the sea. Shakespeare often has ships and shipwrecks in his plays. In *The Tempest* he recreated one

on stage and *Twelfth Night* tells the stories of two survivors.

2 Yes. The Armada tried to invade in 1588, just as Shakespeare was beginning his writing career in London. Shakespeare wrote history plays, like *Henry VI*, that warned audiences, "See what happens when we have a weak monarch? The country is ruined." Queen Elizabeth I was on the throne at the time and not always popular when she was being tough. She would love seeing Shakespeare's plays about weak monarchs; she could say, "A weak king causes more trouble than a tough queen. Support me." As a result she supported the young playwright.

3 No. The Black Death arrived in Britain around 1349. BUT it kept returning regularly and governments closed theatres to prevent it spreading. In *Romeo and Juliet* it is the plague that prevents a message reaching Romeo.

The 1595 audience would understand this well. The plague in London was one of the reasons Shakespeare had *New Place* built in Stratford so he could spend his summers there with his family. Summer in London was a dangerous time for the plague.

4 Yes. Guy Fawkes and some other Catholics tried to blow up James I and his Parliament in 1605. In his play *Macbeth* Shakespeare put in scenes from Scottish history which showed that the true King of Scotland was James I and traitors (like Macbeth or Guy Fawkes) would come to a nasty end. There were also comments on evil characters who said one thing but meant another – "equivocators". Everyone in the audience knew Shakespeare meant James's enemies, the Catholics.

5 No. Witches were never burned at the stake in England – though they were in Scotland and abroad. In

England they were hanged. BUT Shakespeare's audiences would be very interested in witchcraft and witches appear in *Macbeth* and Prospero in *The Tempest* has magical powers. King James I wrote a book on witchcraft and he would enjoy *Macbeth* especially for those scenes. Shakespeare would win the support of James – a very important supporter for any playwright.

6 Yes. Mary Queen of Scots was executed in February 1587, just before Shakespeare began writing. His early plays had scenes with some vicious queens, like Margaret of Anjou in *Henry VI*. She raised an army in Scotland and tried to get help from France for an invasion of England. The audiences of the early 1590s would nod and say, "Just like Mary Queen of Scots."

7 No. Printing presses had been around well over a hundred years, but they didn't do Shakespeare much good.

Shakespeare's plays would be written by hand and copies made for the actors. Shortly before Shakespeare died his friend Ben Jonson arranged to have the scripts gathered together and printed in a book. Shakespeare never lived to see his collected works in print. BUT he did have the advantage of having printed books to read and took a lot of ideas for his plays from history and travel books.

8 Yes. Thomas Walsingham set up a team of spies for Elizabeth I, and the Earl of Salisbury continued to use them under James I. At first their job was to seek out Catholic plots against Protestant Elizabeth. Walsingham's spies proved that the Catholic Mary Queen of Scots wanted to have Elizabeth I killed and take her throne. It was Salisbury's spies who uncovered the Catholic gunpowder plot. Shakespeare never wrote a spy story, but used the idea of spies in some of his plays. In *Hamlet*, for

example, Rosencranz and Guildenstern are supposed to be servants to Prince Hamlet. In fact they were paid to spy on Hamlet and carry secret messages for the English king.

9 Yes. Jewish people had always been treated with suspicion in Elizabeth's England. In 1594 Doctor Roderigo Lopez (who was Jewish) was accused of working for the Spanish and plotting to poison Elizabeth. Hatred for Jewish people flared up again. Christopher Marlowe's play *The Jew of Malta* was a huge success because it showed an evil murderer like Lopez. Shakespeare then seems to have used a similar idea in *The Merchant of Venice*, which is about a cruel Jewish money-lender, Shylock. In fact Shylock is a sad character rather than an evil one, but Elizabethan audiences must have loved to hate him as they said, "Just like Lopez!" The truth is, Lopez was probably innocent!

10 Yes. The Native American princess Pocahontas lived at the same time as Shakespeare and died just a year after him. BUT the story that she saved the life of settler John Smith from her father's warriors is probably untrue. It wasn't published till she and Shakespeare had been dead for eight years.

SHAKESPEARE'S LIFE

WS's Age	Date	History
NOT YET BORN	1349	The Black Death reaches England
	1400	Richard II murdered
	1421	Joan of Arc burned as a witch in France
	1474	Caxton prints the first book in English
	1492	Columbus discovers America
	1509	Henry VIII becomes King
	1558	Elizabeth I becomes queen

WS's Age	WS's Life	Date	History
WS born in Stratford		1564	Scottish rebels fight against Catholic Mary Queen of Scots
4		1568	Mary Queen of Scots flees to England but is arrested by Elizabeth
5	Queen's Theatre Company perform in Stratford. Does WS see them?	1569	Elizabeth faces dangerous rebellion by Catholics but wins
7	WS probably goes to local school	1576	First public playhouse built in London
18	WS possibly working as a school teacher	1581	Francis Drake returns after sailing round the world
19	WS marries Anne Hathaway. The next year daughter Susanna is born.	1582	King James in Scotland kidnapped but released unharmed
21	WS's twins born, Judith and Hamnet	1585	Tough new laws against Catholics meant to protect Elizabeth

WS's Age	WS's Life	Date	History
23	WS arrives in London (probably)	1587	Mary Queen of Scots executed for plotting against Elizabeth
24	WS working as actor (probably)	1588	Spanish Armada beaten by Elizabeth's navy
26	WS's first play is produced – Henry V	1590	
27	WS becoming very popular playwright	1591	Witches attempt to murder James, King of Scotland
28	Theatres closed by plague	1592	Plague kills 15,000 people this year
29	Shakespeare writing poetry while theatres stay closed	1593	Leading playwright Christopher (Kit) Marlowe murdered
30	Theatres re-open	1594	Doctor Roderigo Lopez accused of trying to murder Elizabeth I
32	WS's only son Hamnet dies	1596	Sir Francis Drake dies at sea

WS's Age	WS's Life	Date	History
35	WS share holder in new Globe theatre	1599	Irish rebels throw out English army led by Earl of Essex. Elizabeth I upset!
39	Theatres close again because of plague	1603	Elizabeth I dies; James of Scotland takes over
41	WS writing greatest plays including King Lear	1605	Guy Fawkes and the Gunpowder Plot discovered. Catholic plotters executed
44	WS's granddaughter born	1608	In America English settlers said to be saved by Pocahontas
47	WS writes last great play, The Tempest	1611	The King James Bible published
48	WS mostly retired	1612	Lancashire witches hanged
52	WS dies at Stratford aged 52	1616	Prince Charles made Prince of Wales. As Charles I he will die on the block in 1649

STORY 5: THE MERCHANT OF VENICE

Play number 5 is supposed to be a *comedy* ... but it has some very unpleasant scenes in it. And for one of the main characters it isn't funny at all! This play is called *The Merchant of Venice*.

The "Merchant" is a Christian and his enemy is a Jewish money lender called Shylock. Shakespeare's Shylock tries to explain what it is like to be the victim of Christian torments, but he still ends up defeated and destroyed. To Shakespeare's audience it would be a comedy – they would laugh at the misery of an unpopular money lender ... the way a motorist today might laugh if a Traffic Warden slipped on a banana skin!

But today we know that people aren't wicked just because they have a different colour skin or have a different religion. If Shakespeare had been writing his story now he might have told it more from Shylock's point of view. Perhaps from the point of view of a Jewish newspaper report...

VENETIAN TIMES

Shylock shocker

In a dramatic court case a Jewish money lender has again been denied justice by a strange and inhuman court decision. Money lender Shylock was today in hiding after a legal battle which friends say has left him a "broken and bewildered man".

The matter started last January when the well-known merchant of Venice, Antonio, approached Shylock and asked for a loan of some 3,000 ducats.

OH NO! ANTONIO!!

It seems that the merchant Antonio wanted to lend the money to a friend, Bassanio, who was planning to use it to court the beautiful heiress, Portia of Belmont.

Naturally Shylock knew of Antonio's wealth and asked why he didn't simply use his own money. Antonio explained that he had spent all his money on a fleet of ships with rich cargoes to trade that were sailing across the world. Once the ships returned with the profits then Shylock would be repaid.

Shylock agreed to loan Antonio 3,000 ducats. However, he made the usual "bond" [7] with the merchant of Venice. Normally this would be a house or jewellery or land of the borrower. However, Shylock, being a good natured and sporting person, made a "merry" bond with Antonio which Antonio happily signed. It said that if Antonio failed

[7] A bond is some object of value – if the borrower fails to pay back the money on time, then the lender takes the bond instead.

to repay the 3,000 ducats then Shylock could "cut and take off a whole pound of living flesh from any part of Antonio's body that pleased him".

The reckless merchant had made a bad choice of ships and captains. Before the date for the loan repayment his richest ship was reported as run aground and wrecked. Shylock, naturally, demanded his pound of Christian flesh and took Antonio to court.

Antonio, a young lawyer named Balthasar, agreed that the bond was legal. He invited Shylock to cut off his pound of flesh. Then, as Shylock raised his knife, Balthasar stepped forward and told them that Shylock was not allowed to take one ounce more or less than his pound of flesh.

As Balthasar himself put it, "The scales must not tip even the width of a hair because

SHYLOCK COMES UP AGAINST THE SCALES OF JUSTICE!

But it was a Christian court, and here we see how the strongest case can be overturned when one of our Jewish community is involved.

The defence counsel for

the flesh is over or under a pound. If it does then you die and all of your goods are confiscated." Our readers may think that confiscating his goods would not bother Shylock if he was dead!

However, he has a daughter, Jessica, whom he loves dearly. He is simply making money so that she can be well provided for after his death. Shylock would wish to see his daughter married to a Jewish man and for them to enjoy the money Shylock worked so hard to save.

Shylock objected to this condition. But the Duke, who was acting as judge, *agreed* that this was the law. Furthermore, Balthasar went on, Shylock must not spill one drop of Christian blood as he took that flesh. If Shylock did spill one drop of blood then he himself would face the death penalty.

SHYLOCK WRESTLES WITH THE PROBLEM!

Again the judge agreed with Balthasar's arguments and suddenly it was poor Shylock who was threatened

with death. Shylock said he would forget the debt, but the court insisted he take the flesh or nothing.

BALTHASAR REFUSES TO LET THE MATTER DROP!

Shylock was ready to admit defeat and leave with nothing. But the Christians had not yet finished with him. Shylock was now accused of attempting to murder Antonio! He was found guilty and he was ordered to give up half of his wealth to Venice. Worse was to follow. Shylock was then ordered to become a Christian.

The shattered old man staggered from the court to find still more personal grief awaiting him. Not only had his daughter run off with a Christian, Lorenzo, but she had also stolen Shylock's gold and jewellery savings.

The court ordered that the remaining half of Shylock's wealth should go to his thieving daughter when he dies. Of course, this means that the Christian court takes half of Shylock's money while he's alive and the Christian Lorenzo will get his hands on the other half after the money lender is dead!

How can this be justice? What is the point of an honest Jewish man working, saving and suffering to make a fortune if the courts are going to take it from him so cruelly?

As Shylock himself was heard to say to his tormentors, *I am a Jew. Hath not a Jew eyes … senses affections, passions, fed with the same food, hurt with the same weapons, subject to the same diseases … as a Christian is? If you prick us, do we not bleed? If you tickle us, do we not laugh? If you poison us, do we not die? And if you wrong us, shall we not revenge?*

The answer to these questions, it seems, is "No". A Jew has no right to revenge.

SHYLOCK PLEADS HIS DEFENSE.

After the court case the smirking Antonio and the gloating Bassanio gave an interview to this newspaper. That was when they revealed the most sensational aspect of the whole case.

As we reported, Bassanio used Shylock's loan to help him win the hand of the heiress Portia in marriage. He left the rich Portia to come to the trial in Venice. There he met the devious Balthasar, who defended Antonio and ruined Shylock. When our reporter asked to meet Balthasar he was brought into a room and suddenly Balthasar gripped his lawyer's wig and tugged it off. To the amazement of everyone, Balthasar turned out to be none other than Portia in disguise!

··· "HE" IS A "SHE" !!

This means, of course, that the young wife of Bassanio deceived the judge and lied to the court. Her dishonesty should be punished and Shylock ought to have a new trial with honest lawyers – people who are who they say they are. What chance is there of a re-trial? What chance is there of Shylock getting justice if he suffers a hundred trials? None … because he is Jewish.

His daughter Jessica and her criminal husband Lorenzo should be the ones in the dock. What chance is there of either being brought to trial for the burglary of Shylock's jewels and gold? None … because he is Jewish.

The Christians left the court to celebrate with a party in the moonlit gardens of Venice. Shylock left a poor and broken man to suffer the loneliness of an empty house with empty treasure chests.

Antonio the Merchant of Venice has triumphed . . . while justice in Venice has been the big loser. We weep for Shylock.

SHAKESPEARE'S BLIND DATE

Shakespeare used every trick in the entertainment book to grab his audience's attention. Murder stories, lots of laughs, mysteries, songs, dances, romances ... everything you'd expect to see on television today. You may think Shakespeare didn't write game-shows. Think again!

In *The Merchant of Venice* Bassanio borrows money from Antonio to try to win Portia's love. But it isn't that simple. Portia's father insisted that anyone who wanted to marry her had to pass a test. Choose a casket. The suitor who chooses the casket containing a portrait of Portia wins – she has no say in the matter! For her it's a sort of Blind Date.

Shakespeare shows us three young men each trying to pass the test; it's almost like a game show...

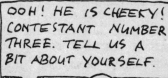

NOW LET'S MEET TONIGHT'S LUCKY LADY WHO'LL GET TO MARRY ONE OF THESE GORGEOUS FELLERS. HERE SHE IS. LET'S HAVE A BIG HAND FOR...... PORTIA!

GOOD EVENING, THRILLA.

MAY I SAY HOW LOVELY YOU LOOK. NOW TELL US A BIT ABOUT YOURSELF.

WELL, THRILLA, MY DAD DIED AND LEFT ME A FORTUNE. BUT HE DIDN'T WANT ME TO MARRY SOMEONE WHO WAS JUST AFTER MY MONEY.

SO WHAT DID HE DO?

HE SAID THAT ANY MAN WHO TAKES MY TEST MUST PROMISE NEVER EVER TO MARRY ANYONE IF HE FAILS MY TEST.

YOU HEAR THAT FELLAS?

YES THRILLA.

NOW, PORTIA, ASK YOUR QUESTION.

THERE ARE THREE CASKETS IN FRONT OF YOU. ONE HOLDS THE KEY TO MY HEART. WHICH ONE WILL YOU CHOOSE?

112

Can you guess who won? And which one would *you* have chosen? Imagine the suspense as the caskets were opened by each contestant in turn.

Answer:
The winner was (surprise, surprise!) Bassanio! Bassanio chose the lead casket because he wasn't fooled by rich appearances. Things that are gold and silver on the outside can be cheap and worthless inside. When Portia's father set the task he didn't want someone to choose his daughter for her money or her appearance. He wanted a man who would see what was inside – her mind.

Having won his prize, Bassanio then had to rush back to Venice to his friend Antonio who was in court, and threatened by Shylock's knife. It was for Bassanio that the Merchant of Venice had gambled his life and it was Antonio who was going to pay.

But it was Portia who came to the rescue. She said she knew a brilliant lawyer who would help Antonio – a Roman lawyer called Balthasar. Balthasar won the case and no one realized that "Balthasar" was in fact Portia in disguise! Well, no one except the audience, of course!

Did you know...?

Actor Charles Macklin was a huge success as Shylock in the early 1800s. Other actors were frightened of the great Macklin and always obeyed his instructions. One night he told an actor, "I will move down the stage and place my foot on this nail. Do not say your words until you see my foot on this nail. Understand?"

"Yes, sir," the terrified young actor replied.

That night Macklin entered, forgot all about the nail, and waited for the young actor to speak. There was a long, long silence on stage. Finally Macklin hissed, "What are you waiting for?"

"For you to put your foot on the nail!"

The great Macklin was so upset he was hardly able to finish playing Shylock that night!

FANTASTIC FACTS 5: VILLAINS OR VICTIMS?

Whenever something goes wrong, people look for someone to blame. But throughout the Middle Ages one group of people took more blame than most. Jewish people.

1 When the Black Death swept through Europe, for example, the Christians didn't understand that it was carried by fleas that lived on rats. Some Christians said it was God's punishment for their sinful ways, but others didn't think they were sinful or that God was so cruel. They looked around for other people to blame. Many blamed the Jewish people.

2 How could the Jews cause plague in a town? They poisoned the drinking water in the wells, the Christians said.

3 The Jews drank the same water and died of the plague too, but the Christians were too stupid to see this.

4 What could be done about the Jews? Kill them; men, women and children.

5 In Germany 6,000 Jews were massacred in Mainz in the year of the Black Death, 1349.

6 Others committed suicide by setting fire to themselves in their houses rather than face the mobs.

7 In Erfurt not one of the 3,000 Jewish inhabitants was left alive.

8 Another problem was that Christians were not allowed to make money from money lending. If a Christian

wanted money then he or she had to go to a Jewish money lender. Some people must have taken part in massacres of Jews because it meant the money they owed did not have to be repaid!

9 By Shakespeare's time the English Jews were accepted until someone accused a Jewish doctor of trying to poison Queen Elizabeth. The old hatred flared up again. A play called *The Jew of Malta* by Christopher Marlowe showed a Jewish man as a monster and the play was a huge success.

10 William Shakespeare cashed in on this public feeling by writing about a villainous Jewish money lender, called Shylock, in his play *The Merchant of Venice*.

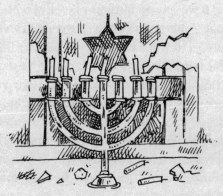

STORY 6: ROMEO AND JULIET

At number 6 we have a famous play. Everyone's heard of the two main characters even if they've never heard of Shakespeare! They are Romeo and Juliet.

William Shakespeare wrote plays but he didn't usually think of the original stories. In 1562 (two years before Shakespeare was born) a poem was written called *The Tragical History of Romeus and Juliet*. The poem was very popular and Shakespeare took the story as the basis of his own play *Romeo and Juliet*.

Since Shakespeare's play was first performed there have been many other versions of the same story of hopeless love between two young people who should be enemies. A musical was made about two lovers from rival street gangs in New York; it was a singing and dancing *Romeo and Juliet* called *West Side Story*. In the 1970s, a film was made at a time when Russia and America were close to war. A Russian boy and an American girl fell in love. The film was called *Romanov and Juliet*.

So there's nothing new about taking the story and presenting it in a different way ... as a poem, as a play, as a film, as a musical and *now* as a photo love story!

PLAY DEAD

Romeo Montague: Young, handsome hero. Madly in love ... with Rosaline! That is until he meets Juliet, of course. Good with swords and words. If he lived today he'd be into boy-racer cars, drinking lager and supporting Manchester United Football Club.

Juliet Capulet: Romantic teenager (around 14 years old). Not in love with anyone. Until she meets Romeo, of course. If she lived today she'd be into pop music, discos, clothes and endless phone conversations with her mates.

Mercutio: Romeo's cousin. Hates Capulets, hates wimps, hates women and probably hates himself. If he lived today he'd be into joy-riding, mugging old ladies, drinking till he falls senseless in the gutter and picking his nose.

Tybalt: Juliet's cousin. Hates Montagues, train-spotters, his dad and lettuce. If he lived today he'd be seen hanging around on street corners, picking his finger nails with a knife, shouting rude things at girls walking past and peeing on his dad's best rose bush.

ONCE UPON A TIME THERE WERE TWO YOUNG PEOPLE.....

I'M ROMEO MONTAGUE......AND I HATE THE CAPULET FAMILY.

I'M JULIET CAPULET ...AND I HATE THE MONTAGUES!

BUT THEN THEY MET...

COR! SHE'S GORGEOUS

WHAT A HUNK!

ROMEO'S FRIEND MERCUTIO WARNED HIM ......

WHILE JULIET'S COUSIN, TYBALT, WARNED HER...

SO THAT NIGHT ROMEO WENT ROUND TO JULIET'S WINDOW....

121

ROMEO TOLD JULIET TO JOIN HIM BUT SHE HAD TROUBLE WITH HER DAD.....

Did you know....?

Audiences do not always sit and watch a Shakespeare play in silence. Many people treat the plays a bit like a pantomime and enjoy shouting at the actors. This is a great problem when the actors are trying to do a serious play. In an 1813 performance of *Romeo and Juliet* someone threw a cockerel on stage and it strutted around at Romeo's feet while the audience howled with laughter. At the end of the play a character called Paris who has been killed by Romeo was lying dead on the stage. An orange was thrown from the audience and landed smack on his nose. The corpse stood up and walked off the stage! Finally, as Romeo made his dying speech the restless audience cried, "Get on with it! Why don't you die?"

FANTASTIC FACTS 6: FOUL WORD-PLAY

William Shakespeare used about 17,000 words in his plays and almost 2,000 of those were words that had never been recorded before. That's not to say he *invented* all 2,000 … but if he hadn't used them they'd probably have been lost forever.

He also put words together and came up with new phrases like "foul play" and words like "laughable".

PESTER YOUR PARENTS

Ask: "Which of the following words or phrases were first used by William Shakespeare?"
  1 A tower of strength
  2 Assassination
  3 Countless
  4 To the manner born
  5 Dwindle
  6 I must be cruel to be kind
  7 Fancy-free
  8 Bag and baggage
  9 Vanish into thin air
  10 Flesh and blood

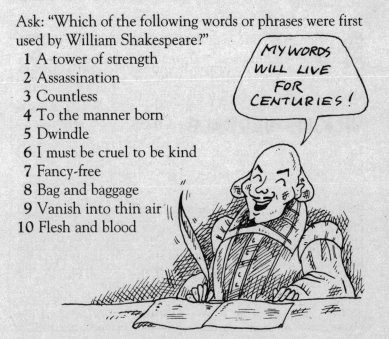

Answer:
All of them are first recorded in Shakespeare manuscripts.

Of course, he had his failures too! Here are the ten best words that *didn't* catch on:

1 abruption
2 anhungry [8]
3 appertainments
4 cadent
5 conflux
6 protractive
7 questrist
8 tortive
9 ungenitured
10 vastidity

Even though no one ever uses these words today you can learn them and impress your teachers. It doesn't matter if you don't know what they mean – pretend you do know. No one else will understand them!

VICIOUS VERBALS

In *Romeo and Juliet* Shakespeare probably discovered how much audiences enjoyed good fights. But there are more ways to fight than one. You can fight with words as well as weapons. In *Romeo and Juliet* cross words lead to crossed swords and death. A fight starts in the opening act simply because a servant of the Capulet family bites his thumb as he looks at a Montague servant. Did *you* know that was a great insult in Tudor times?

[8] A popular question with language students is "How many words end in NGRY?" The word "hungry" is one and the word "angry", is a second. But Shakespeare's "anhungry", meaning hungry is still in some dictionaries.

In every Shakespeare play you can find wonderful insults that people still enjoy watching or even *saying* today. You may not understand what a "prating mountebank" means,[9] but it sounds wonderful if you can remember it and call your worst enemy that!

In fact Shakespeare mixed his words so well that you can make up new insults from his. Here are the ten best Shakespeare insults. See if you can match the correct word on the left with its partner on the right. It doesn't matter if you get the answers wrong, you may discover some wonderful *new* insults as you try. "Bloodsucker of caterpillars" looks a rather pleasant thing to call someone who has upset you!

A

1 taffeta

2 scurvy

3 red-tailed

4 threadbare

5 mad-headed

6 fat

7 false

8 bloodsucker of

9 scolding

10 deformed

B

1 lump

2 ape

3 chuff

4 bumble-bee

5 punk

6 juggler

7 crookback

8 caterpillars

9 sleeping men

10 lord

[9] Actually it means "chattering cheat".

127

Answers:
Shakespeare wrote these insults as:
1 taffeta punk
2 scurvy lord
3 red-tailed bumble-bee
4 threadbare juggler
5 mad-headed ape
6 fat chuff
7 false caterpillars
8 bloodsucker of sleeping men
9 scolding crookback
10 deformed lump

STORY 7: JULIUS CAESAR

This story is one of Shakespeare's *history* plays – *Julius Caesar*.

The Elizabethan playwright Ben Jonson said that Shakespeare knew little Latin and less Greek. In other words he wasn't very well educated in Stratford.

So how could Shakespeare write plays about great Romans like Julius Caesar if he couldn't read the Latin histories? The answer is that he read translations from the Latin into English. Then he changed the history to suit his plays!

For example, Julius Caesar was murdered on the 15th March, buried on the 17th and his nephew, Octavius, arrived in Rome two months later. In Shakespeare's play *Julius Caesar* these things *all* happen on 15th March. The play is more exciting because things seem to happen more quickly. Great theatre, terrible history!

The real "hero" of Julius Caesar is in fact Brutus. As in most tragedies most of the leading characters die. If Brutus had left a suicide note then it might have untangled the story for us...

The revenge of Caesar's spirit

These are the final words of my life. I, Brutus
plan to kill myself. My most loyal slave will
hold my sword and I shall fall upon it.

My enemies say I have no guts. I'll show
them guts. All over the floor.

If I live, then my enemies will only capture
me and claim the glory. They will also make
sure I die very slowly and very painfully. I'm
no coward. I'm not afraid to die. I just can't
bear the thought of that lot enjoying
themselves while I do it. I can just see
them now......... eating grapes and drinking
sherbet while I roast over a grill
or get smothered in honey and
eaten to death by ants. I can't stand ants.

But, as I was saying. my enemies
don't deserve the glory of capturing me
and killing me. They haven't defeated me. I
have been defeated by a dead man. I am
haunted by the spirit of Julius Caesar
and the only escape is to kill myself.

Julius Caesar was a great man, make
no mistake. Bald, ugly and very big-headed.
I am also much more modest
about my abilities. I am just as good
in battle and have more hair. Still,
I have to admit, he won great
victories for the Roman people; he
brought us wealth and power across
the world. But Rome is ruled by the

JULIUS
CAESAR

people. They elect their leaders. Caesar was planning to make himself Emperor of Rome. He was planning to take all that power for himself. He had to die so the people could be free.

He also had to die so I could become the leader, of course. That's why I agreed to take part in the bold plot to murder him.

Someone had to be ready to take his place when he died and it might as well be someone noble, brave, modest and hairy like me. I'll never forget that night when Cassius, that thin and cold man visited me as the sky was being torn apart by a storm. I am not afraid of thunder, you understand. I was simply looking for a missing nut that rolled under the couch.

ME

CASSIUS

"Scared of the storm?" Cassius asked as he marched into my room without knocking.

I wriggled out from under the couch. "Looking for a nut, old boy," I explained.

"Funny you should mention that," he laughed. "I know where there are twenty of them! Twenty nuts, all crazy to stick a knife in Julius Caesar!"

"Must be a big knife," I gasped.

"No," Cassius said with a patient sigh. "Twenty knives. One each."

"Twenty knives!" I cried. "You could kill him!"

Cassius nodded his thin head. "That is the general idea, Brutus," he murmured.

"Kill my friend, Julius Caesar? The noblest Roman of them all? The great and undefeated general? The hero of the Roman people? How could you even think of doing such a thing?" I cried.

Cassius shrugged. "Thought we might give his job to you, old chap."

"When do we kill him?" I smiled.

"Tomorrow. We stab him in the forum."

"I'd rather stab him in the back," I said. And so it was agreed. They would stab him — and I'd stick the odd knife into him when I was sure he was too dead to fight back. After all, it wouldn't do to risk the life of Brutus, the new leader, would it?

Caesar was my friend. I loved him, but I love the Roman people more. I agreed to the murder, so long as Caesar's greatest supporter, Mark Antony, should not die at the same time. After all, I argued, Caesar was the evil that we needed to cut out.

Later that night I met my fellow conspirators who were unhappy at letting Mark Antony live. I forced them to agree with me. That was my first mistake. I see now that Mark Antony should have died at the same time. Cassius was right.

MARK ANTONY

You will know about the assassination, of course. Caesar made his way to a meeting with us and was warned by his wife that he was in danger. A fortune teller in the street even warned him, but he ignored them all.

MRS CAESAR

"Beware the Ides of March!" the sooth-sayer sooth-said as sooth sayers often do.

"That's tomorrow," Caesar nodded. "Thanks for the warning, pal," Caesar said.

"Nah! It's today mate!" the sooth-sayer sooth-said.

"Look, chum you just happen to be talking to the man who invented the Roman Calendar. I am Julius Caesar. They named July after me."

"That your name then?" the sooth-sayer sooth-asked. "Julia?"

"Look, mush. It's the 14th March today."

"It's the 15th!" the sooth-sayer sooth-argued. "But if you think it's the 14th then fine. In that case beware the day-before-the-Ides-of-March!" the sooth-sayer sooth cried.

When Caesar arrived we drew our daggers and each tried to plunge them into him.

As he was dying, Caesar looked at me and his face was twisted with pain. Not the pain from a score of stab wounds. But the pain of knowing that his "honest" friend was also going to betray him. "You too, Brutus?" he asked, and covered his face with his arm so he could not see me strike the final blow.

We allowed Mark Antony to speak at Caesar's funeral. Letting him live was our first mistake. This was our second mistake. The Roman people were whipped into a fury by his speech. We had killed Caesar for love of those people, but they didn't seem to understand! They turned on us and would have murdered us too! I fled with Cassius while Mark Antony formed an army to catch and punish the assassins. He was joined by Caesar's nephew, Octavius.

One by one the assassins were caught and killed. We were hunted like foxes and haunted by the dreadful deed we'd done. We gathered an army among Caesar's enemies and tried to defend ourselves. But we were not united the way Mark Antony and Octavius were united. Their hatred for Caesar's killers drove them on.

OCTAVIUS

Cassius quarrelled with me. It was a silly quarrel. He was upset because I was right and he was wrong. Old Cassius even offered me his dagger so I could kill him as I had killed Caesar. "Go on. Stick it in. Twist it around a bit. You'll enjoy that, won't you?" I could not kill another man in cold blood.

Anyway, I wanted to stop running, to turn and fight at Philippi. Cassius warned me that our forces were too weak but I wouldn't listen.

I didn't even listen when Julius Caesar himself warned me. For it was his ghost that visited me the night before the battle. "I will see you at Philippi, Brutus," he warned.

"You planning to be there then?" I asked.

"I'll be there, sunshine, to watch you

suffer defeat."

"Well, if you know the result, there's not a lot of point in me turning up for the battle, is there?" I asked.

"It's your fate," he said.

Now for a moment, I thought he said, "It's your 'feet'." I looked down and saw I'd forgotten to put me slippers on. When I looked up he was gone. Ghosts are like that.

And, sure enough, we lost. Personally I wouldn't have bothered turning up, knowing the result in advance as I did, but Cassius was keen to see me there. A bit of moral support, as it were.

When Cassius heard the battle was lost he threw himself on his sword. But here's a funny thing. Hilarious, in fact. The report that we had lost the battle was wrong! Cassius died because a messenger made a mistake! But without Cassius to lead his forces the battle has finally turned against us. Antony's army is drawing near and so is the time of my death.

Caesar, you were truly a great man. But no man is greater than the Roman people. You had to die. You had to. Now I am coming to join you, Caesar.

The sword is ready. The spirit of dead Caesar is waiting.

Yours truly,

Brutus

P.S. Just sent the slave to check the blade was sharp. Don't want to have any accidents do we?

P.P.S. Just sent the slave for some wine. My mouth is dry and I can't speak my famous last words.

P.P.P.S. Just sent the slave for some roasted dormice on toast. I don't want to die on an empty stomach. Very unhealthy.

P.P.P.P.S. Slave here. Got fed up with the boss putting off and putting off. I said, "Look at that crow!" When he looked up I stabbed him. Got it over with. His famous last words? "Infamy! Infamy! You all have it in-for-me!"

Did you know...?

Shakespeare didn't just change historical events to suit the action. He also made careless mistakes about Roman life and didn't seem to care.

In *Julius Caesar*:

- Shakespeare's characters wore hats, cloaks and doublets just as the Elizabethan audience did, BUT ... the Romans would have worn *togas*!
- Shakespeare's Brutus finds the page of a book that he has marked, BUT ... the real Brutus would have read from a parchment *scroll*.
- Shakespeare's Brutus listens to the clock chiming the hours, BUT ... chiming clocks would not be invented for another 1,500 years!

FANTASTIC FACTS 7: WHO WROTE SHAKESPEARE?

Shakespeare wrote about great Roman characters like Julius Caesar, Mark Antony and Coriolanus. He also wrote wonderful poetry. Over the years since Shakespeare's death, some academics and professors believed that a glover's son from Stratford could *not* have had the brains or the education to write these plays.

Someone else wrote them, they claim, and then stuck the name of a simple actor on the play. The actor was William Shakespeare, but the real writer of the plays was someone else. Who?

A priest called the Reverend James Wilmot started the trouble about a hundred years after the death of Shakespeare. The Rev. went to Stratford to investigate old records. He couldn't find any letters by Shakespeare, any books owned by him, or any mentions of "Shakespeare the play writer" by other Stratford people of the time. Wilmot also couldn't believe that a glover's son like Shakespeare could go on to become a favourite of a queen and a king. He started the suspicion that Shakespeare's plays weren't written by William Shakespeare.

137

American Delia Bacon was even more snobbish. She said Will was, "A stupid, ignorant third-rate play-actor from a dirty, doggish group of players."

Whodunit?

Here are the top ten possibles:

1 Queen Elizabeth I

Claim: The queen loved drama. But women and upper-class people could not be seen to write something as "common" as a stage play. She had to disguise her efforts by giving them to a young actor she fancied, William Shakespeare. Elizabeth had the education necessary to write the plays and backed Shakespeare's theatre company for many years. Computer experts have matched Elizabeth's portrait with Shakespeare's and say they are the same person!

Against: She continued writing the plays for eight years after her death. A clever trick if you can manage it.

Score: 1/10

2 King James I

Claim: The king was fanatical about witchcraft and about his own right to the throne. The play *Macbeth* is about witchcraft and kingship. Who better to write the play than James the expert? He put a lot of his own money into Shakespeare's plays ... so that Shakespeare would produce the plays written by the king?

Against: Shakespeare's plays were being written in 1590 while James was still in Scotland. And James wasn't all that bright.

Score: 2/10

3 Anthony Bacon

Claim: Brother of the famous Francis (see number 8). Anthony visited the French king's court in the early 1590s. When *Love's Labour's Lost* was performed in 1593 there were characters called Berowne, Dumain and Longaville, almost the same names as French lords that Anthony would have been mixing with.

Against: He wasn't in England much when the plays were being performed.

Score: 3/10

4 Henry Wriothesley, Earl of Southampton

Claim: A brilliant student who went to Cambridge University when he was just sixteen and a rich playboy who gave a lot of money to Will Shakespeare. Shakespeare is supposed to have written poems like *Venus and Adonis* for young Henry. But what if Henry wrote the plays and Shakespeare agreed to have his name put on them?

Against: Henry enjoyed good living too much. Would he have had the energy to write plays?

Score: 4/10

5 The Earl of Rutland

Claim: The Earl knew Shakespeare and there are records that he paid Shakespeare money. Money for Shakespeare's help in producing the Earl's plays? The Earl had been to several of the places where the plays are set – Venice, Verona, Padua – whereas William Shakespeare probably hadn't. The Earl even went to the Danish court just before *Hamlet, Prince of Denmark* was written.

He died in 1613 when the last Shakespearean play was written.

Against: There is no proof that the Earl of Rutland ever wrote a play.

Score: 5/10

6 William Stanley, Earl of Derby

Claim: A scholar dug up an old letter that said the Earl of Derby was "busy penning comedies for the common players". There is no record of a Stanley or Derby play ever being performed. So, if they weren't performed as Stanley plays, were they performed as Shakespeare plays? Derby had been to France as a young man and met some of the real people who later appeared in the Shakespeare plays.

Against: There may be no record of a Stanley play being performed because they never were performed. Lots of people write plays that don't get performed. They are just too awful!

Score: 6/10

7 Edward de Vere, Earl of Oxford [10]

Claim: There were letters that said he wrote plays but, like the Earl of Derby, no list of his plays survives.

---

[10]Let's hope Oxford didn't write the plays. He was not a nice man. He murdered a kitchen lad with his sword in a fit of temper and gave his poor wife a very hard time.

However, one of his descendants now travels around the world giving lectures on how Oxford came to write the plays. There are many supporters of the theory that Oxford wrote the plays.

Against: He died in 1604 and, like Elizabeth, must have written the greatest Shakespeare plays from the grave. Maybe he used a ghost writer!

Score: 7/10

8 Sir Francis Bacon

Claim: The writer of Shakespeare's plays knew a lot about law and a lot about the French king's court. Bacon's brother, Anthony, had been to the French court and written home to Francis. Bacon's father had been Elizabeth's Lord Keeper and his mother had been related to Elizabeth's chief minister. Bacon was a poet.

Against: Bacon had no experience of the theatre.[11]

Score: 8/10

[11]Bacon's name has given rise to a lot of cruel jokes through the years ... "If Bacon wrote the plays, pigs might fly." ... "The play *Hamlet, Prince of Denmark* was a piece of Danish Bacon" ... or Bacon put the "ham" in *Hamlet* ... or, if Bacon said he wrote the plays he was telling porkies ... You know the sort of thing. You'll be pleased to know you will not find such dreadful jokes in this book.

9 Christopher Marlowe

Claim: A brilliant young playwright and a huge success when William Shakespeare arrived in London. However, he was in trouble for his spying activities. He had to fake his own death to save his life. In order to keep writing plays he produced them under Shakespeare's name. Shakespeare was well paid so he didn't mind taking the glory.[12]

Against: There is too much evidence to show that Marlowe WAS murdered in 1592.

Score: 9/10

10 William Shakespeare

Claim: Everybody said he wrote the plays, including people like Ben Jonson and other playwrights that he was competing with.

Against: Not a lot.

Score: 10/10

The problem of "Who wrote Shakespeare?" was sensibly solved in the 1940s by a professor who paid a spiritualist

[12]A scholar got permission to dig up the grave of Marlowe's protector, hoping to find new manuscripts. In fact he didn't find new plays – he didn't even find a body! He found a coffin full of sand! A shore sign of something?

to get in touch with the ghosts of Shakespeare, Oxford and Bacon. The spirits told her that they *all* wrote the plays! Shakespeare did the plots, Oxford worked on the characters and Bacon polished the poetry.

Dead men tell no lies, but spiritualists sometimes do! Believe that if you want.

Did you know…?
Shakespeare's longest word is:
"Honorificabilitudinitatibus."
Rearrange the letters and you get the Latin phrase, *Hi ludi F. Baconis nati tuiti orbi*. In English this means, "These plays, the children of F. Bacon, are preserved for the world." Some writers have used this to prove that Bacon wrote the plays.

I AM STILL NOT CONVINCED!

STORY 8: THE TAMING OF THE SHREW

Play number 8 is about the age-old battle between men and women and who is the boss.

Shakespeare had a problem with women characters. Women were not allowed to act on stage. So, whenever he wanted a female character he had to dress a boy in a woman's costume and a wig.

The boys were very good for their age, but as soon as their voices broke they had to give up playing women's parts and new young actors had to be trained. So the best parts and the strongest characters were usually written for men. There are very few good parts for actresses in Shakespeare's plays. And the women who are there are often weak or the victims of men, and this is not popular with women in the twentieth century!

The worst play from a woman's point of view is probably *The Taming of the Shrew*. The story is about a strong woman who is bullied until she becomes a quiet, obedient wife.

If there had been newspapers in Shakespeare's day, and if they had women reporters, how would they have reviewed *The Taming of the Shrew*?

Shrew shocker

13th September 1593

Mr Shakespeare's latest play opened at *The Theatre* playhouse last night. The men in the audience cheered as they saw brave Katherine Minola's spirit broken by the evil Petruchio. Women watched in horrified silence.

The play, set in Italy, opens with a drunken tinker called Sly being found by a group of noblemen. As a joke, they tell Sly that he is a wealthy man who has been asleep for fifteen years. The noblemen say they will show him a play that will cure his madness. The play is *The Taming of the Shrew*.

The unfortunate "shrew" is Katherine Minola, a young woman who has had to watch as her younger sister, Bianca, has been spoiled for years by their weak father. Now the father won't let Bianca marry until Katherine is married off first. The problem is that Katherine is very sharp-tongued and argumentative. She bullies her own sister and will have none of the husbands her father suggests. No one will marry her, even though her father offers a large sum of money. No one, that is, until the half crazy Petruchio appears. He decides to take the money and tame the shrewish Katherine, whether she likes the idea or not.

What can Katherine do? If she refuses to marry Petruchio, then Bianca will lose the young man she wants to marry. Bravely Katherine sacrifices her own happiness to make her spoilt sister happy. She agrees to marry the arrogant, boastful Petruchio. It is a dreadful mistake on her part.

Petruchio not only forces Katherine into marriage but disgraces himself at the wedding, arriving on a broken-down old horse, dressed in badly-fitting clothes. He swears at the priest, throws wine over the poor man and then kisses Katherine so hard the echo of the kiss rings around the church.

Katherine is by now confused and afraid. She is also very hungry but Petruchio insists on leaving for their new home *before* the wedding feast. He sends her to bed with no food when they arrive at the house. His excuse is that it is badly cooked – and cruelly makes her thank him, next day, for the food she didn't eat! Then he sends away her fine new clothes because, he says, they are not good enough for her.

The poor woman says he is trying to make her a puppet; in fact it is worse. He is training her like a falcon, a wild bird that is captured and starved until it comes to hand when its master orders it.

The starved and defeated woman is finally made to look an utter fool. To please Petruchio and to survive she will say anything. She swears that the sun is the moon just to make him happy. She even agrees that an old man is a young girl.

When they return to her father's house Katherine now tells her sister, Bianca,

that a good wife is one who obeys her husband. Her speech at the end of the play is quite outrageous! She tells Bianca that her husband is "thy lord, thy life, thy keeper" who deserves "love and true obedience".

Nonsense, Mr Shakespeare. That is the sort of thing that only the men in the audience want to hear and want to believe. Would you dare tell our Queen Elizabeth this sort of nonsense?

Women have rights too, Mr Shakespeare, and your play is a crime against them. And what is more, Mr Shakespeare, it is not even funny.

Our agony Aunt writes and disagrees with our reviewer:

We have a queen on the throne, so we should expect the lives of women to improve. Sadly, in the reign of Elizabeth this has not been the case. The story of Katherine Minola might be fiction, but cases like hers are still common although they are not as common as they used to be.

A recent visitor to our shores, a twenty-five-year-old German called Thomas Platter claims that women in England are better off than their sisters in Europe! We may wonder how they can be worse off, but he assures us they are! Here is an extract from his book, published recently:

The women folk of England, who have mostly blue-grey eyes and are fair and pretty, have far more freedom than women in other lands. Women more often than men are to be found in the ale-houses for enjoyment. If only one woman is invited she will bring three or four other women along and they will gaily drink a health to one another. They often stroll out in gorgeous clothes and are specially fond of great ruffs which they starch blue. The men must put up with this and dare not punish them, indeed the good wives often beat their men. An English proverb sums it up: "England is a woman's paradise and a servant's prison."[13]

---

[13]Quote from actual publication by Platter though this was written in October 1599, some six years after *The Taming of the Shrew* was first produced.

This is a great exaggeration, of course, but it does give us a clue to Mr Shakespeare's play. It is a joke. Men are in fact afraid of their women. The only way they can strike back is by writing plays in which men are seen to bully and starve women into submission.

In writing this play Mr Shakespeare is NOT showing that men despise women. It shows that they in fact FEAR women. If you suffer from being married to a Petruchio, then it is good to remember that: a bully is AFRAID of his victim. *The Taming of the Shrew* is how Mr Shakespeare would LIKE to treat his wife. Perhaps, when he next goes home to Stratford, Mrs Shakespeare will show him that women are neither shrewish nor there to be tamed.

A funny little play, Mr Shakespeare, but it could only have been written by a frightened man . . . and the joke is on you.

The Taming of the Shrew is a difficult play to stage in the modern theatre. No matter how the play is performed it shows women being unjustly controlled by men.

Did you know...?
Although women were banned from appearing on stage, some tried to do it. One of the most famous was a criminal known as Moll Cutpurse. Moll was arrested for appearing on stage, dressed in men's clothes and singing rude songs while playing the lute.

FANTASTIC FACTS 8: SHAKESPEARE'S AUDIENCES

Shakespeare knew what his audiences liked and was popular because he provided it, but the audience often had quite a hard time!

There were no seats in front of the stage in Shakespeare's playhouses, so the audience would have to stand for two, three or even four hours to see a performance. If they grew bored they would just talk among themselves or throw food on the stage. If they were excited they would scream at the actors, cheer their heroes or swear and boo at the villains.

DON'T YOU HATE IT WHEN THAT HAPPENS ?!

Things did not change a great deal until this century. Nowadays people are expected to behave quietly and politely in the theatre. It hasn't always been that way!

SUFFERING SPECTATORS

1 William Shakespeare was one of the best-known playwrights in Elizabethan England. But audiences weren't so interested in *playwrights* before he came along. They were interested in the *performers*. The star actors were like the pop stars of today. In 1578, ten years before Shakespeare started writing, an audience gathered to see the famous comic actor Richard Tarleton. Too many fans tried to crowd into London's Guildhall to see him

and the huge doors were broken off their iron hinges as they struggled to get in.

2 A Welsh character in *Henry V*, called Fluellen, has to eat a leek in one scene. In a New York production of 1875 the actor couldn't stand leeks and, since he was at the front of the stage, he couldn't just *pretend* to eat the leek. A clever stage manager made a cardboard leek and filled the end with an apple. The actor ate the apple. BUT ... one night the cardboard leek was lost. The actor was forced to eat a real leek. He did this ... but it made him so ill he vomited over the front row of the audience!

3 In London's Covent Garden theatre in 1801 the audiences enjoyed taking drink into the theatre and watching Shakespeare's plays as they became more and more drunk. An actor playing the role of a villain was really unpopular with the audience ... so they kidnapped him and held him in the front row. The rest of the play had to go on without him!

4 Riots in theatres were common in Shakespeare's time. The audience often threw fruit at the actors, which could be a problem. But on one occasion a large bottle bounced off an actor's hat as he tried to perform Shakespeare's *Richard III*. He picked it up and refused to go back on stage. The audience were only calmed down when the army was called in and six guardsmen with bayonets cleared the trouble-makers out.

THAT'S IT !! I'M OFF HOME LUVVIE!

5 Even the most popular actors suffered from rioting crowds. John Kemble's theatre was burned down, so he rebuilt it and started to perform Shakespeare plays again. But he said he had to increase the prices in order to pay for the new plays. The audience didn't believe him and the hisses and yells and groans from the audience drove him from the stage. This went on every night till Kemble agreed to lower the prices again and apologized. The audience replied by unrolling a banner. It said, "We are satisfied."

HISSSS..

GET OFF!

BOO!!

ALL RIGHT, YA MEAN OLD RABBLE! YOU'VE MADE YOUR POINT!

6 David Garrick changed a lot of Shakespeare customs. For example, he stopped the rich spectators sitting on the stage during a performance. The door to the theatre was guarded by two soldiers to prevent excited fans reaching the great man back stage. But one night Garrick's performance of *King Lear* was so powerful one of the guards fainted. The kind actor gave the man a gold coin. The next night another guard fainted ... and waited for his coin. Garrick wasn't fooled, because the second night he'd been acting in a *comedy!*

7 Some members of the audience would do anything to get close to the action. A fan of Shakespeare's plays called Sol Smith crept into the theatre early and hid in a box at the side of the stage. He pulled down the lid leaving just a small crack and had a wonderful view of *Richard III*, until four actors picked up the box and carried it onto the stage. It wasn't simply a box that he was hiding in, it was a coffin for use on the stage! Sol gave a small groan from inside the coffin, the terrified actors dropped it and ran. Some say the actors never returned to the theatre and one even became a priest!

8 Sometimes audiences can try to be helpful. In a performance of *Hamlet* an actor had no time to learn the part of Osric. He simply slipped a copy of the play into his hat and read it. But at a dramatic point in the play he stopped and squinted into the hat. There was a word he couldn't make out. A kind member of the audience realized what was happening and called, "You spell it out, pal, we'll tell you what it is!"

9 Modern audiences don't always know how to behave at a Shakespeare play. In a 1970 performance in a theatre in the north-east of England the audience was 2,000 school children. They seemed to have the idea that you should applaud when a character died. Julius Caesar died and the audience burst into long and loud applause. The trouble is an awful lot of characters die in *Julius Caesar*. Every one got long, loud applause. The two-and-a-half hour-play went on three hours and most of the audience missed their buses back to school! Perhaps that's what they wanted?

10 On a visit to the USA in 1826, William Charles Macready became involved in a rivalry with the American actor Edwin Forrest. By 1849 supporters of Forrest were trying to wreck Macready's performances. On 2nd April in Cincinnati someone threw half a dead sheep on stage. Perhaps the audience wanted to see *As Ewe Like It*? Then on 10th May a riot broke out in a New York theatre. During the riot 22 people were killed and 36 were injured. More corpses than a Shakespeare tragedy! Macready just managed to escape with his life. He retired two years later and suffered no more ram raids.

STORY 9: MACBETH

The second most popular play of Shakespeare is his shortest and one of his spookiest. It is called *Macbeth* and Shakespeare wrote it in 1606 to please the new king, James I, who was also James VI of Scotland.

James was fascinated by witchcraft and believed firmly in the power of witches. A writer called Reginald Scot wrote *The Discovery of Witchcraft* in 1584 and argued that witchcraft was nothing more than a series of conjuring tricks and lies. King James was furious! He wrote his own book, *Demonology*, in which he refuted all of Scot's arguments.

James was also keen to continue the royal support of Shakespeare's plays and his theatre. The king spent money like water and gave plenty to the actor's company. Shakespeare was so pleased that he wrote *Macbeth* especially for the king – a play about a Scottish king and about witchcraft.

Shakespeare wrote *Macbeth* in 1606 when he was a very experienced playwright. Long poems in the Elizabethan age had used a regular rhythm or beat and were copied from old Latin poems. There were five of these "beats" to the line. They sounded:

di-DUM, di-DUM, di-DUM, di-DUM, di-DUM

So, a line from *Romeo and Juliet* written around 1594 went:

Did MY heart LOVE till NOW forSWEAR it SIGHT
I NEver SAW true BEAUty TILL this NIGHT

After a while that sort of beat becomes monotonous and sends you to sleep! But, by the time he wrote *Macbeth* Shakespeare was not too bothered about keeping this strict rhythm all the way through his plays.

Poetry usually rhymed, such as "sight" and "night". Poetry in the plays didn't usually rhyme, so it was known as "blank" verse.

If the story of *Macbeth* were told as a blank verse poem it might sound like this...

The ballad of Big Mac[14]

The lightning flashed as red as blood across
The purple morning sky. It lit the little
Group of shapeless, gruesome figures
As they huddled round a pot and chanted,

Double, double toil and trouble: fire, burn; and,
cauldron, bubble . . .
Cool it with a baboon's blood, then the charm is firm and
good.[15]

The heath was empty as the witches worked
Their spells. It seemed that every living thing
Had fled for safety from the moor or lay
In hiding underneath the dripping rocks.

Until a man appeared and splashed along
The lonely, stony path across the moor.
A man in leather armour with a sword
That carried scars and stains from recent battles.

[14]It's great to read out loud!
[15]The spells are in Shakespeare's words.

The witches chuckled and gave toothless smiles
And stirred and stirred and mumbled frantic curses.
"By the pricking of my thumbs," one screeched,
"Something wicked this way comes. Macbeth!"

The soldier marching down the path had stopped.
He smelled the witches' evil brew and saw
The smoke rise up into the watery air.
And then he heard his name screeched out,
"Macbeth!"

He stepped across the heather. Drew his sword.
He looked down in the hollow in the heather
Where the ugly, writing creatures chanted.
Macbeth shuddered as he heard their spell.

Fillet of a fenny snake, in the cauldron boil and bake.
Eye of newt and toe of frog, wool of bat and tongue of
dog
Adder's fork, and blind-worm's sting, lizard's leg, and
howlet's wing –
For a charm of powerful trouble, like a hell-broth, boil
and bubble.

Something crooked, like a finger, pointed
At Macbeth. The creature's face was hidden
In the filthy folds of its foul-smelling robe.
From that shadowed hood a voice hissed, soft.

"Macbeth, we welcome you upon the heath.
Macbeth, the man who will be Scotland's king!"
The other creatures laughed and bowed down low.
"Macbeth," they wailed, "the man who will be king!"

To be the king was more than he had dreamed;
"So tell me how you know this!" Macbeth cried.
But as he moved towards the bat-black shapes
They vanished in the steaming, smoke-choked air.

The soldier went back to his castle grey
Where in the torchlit halls his waiting wife
Gave him the news that Scotland's ageing king,
Old Duncan, would arrive to stay that very night.

The Lady of Macbeth she smiled and showed
Her teeth, as glittering as a hungry wolf.
"The king may come," she hissed,
"But he will never leave these walls alive!"

The Lord Macbeth then plotted with his wife
The way to murder Duncan as he slept.
They drugged the wine and sent his guards to sleep,
Then stole their daggers for the wicked deed.

The cruel Macbeth crept in the old man's room
His heart was cold and steely as the knives.
He slaughtered Duncan as the old man slept.
Then killed the guards so they would take the blame.

The lords of Scotland wept for their dead king –
Then chose the man to take his royal throne.
They chose the bravest soldier in the land;
They chose Macbeth, assassin, as their king.

So murdering Macbeth began to rule
With scheming wife and witches at his back.
When rebels in the land began to fight,
Then Macbeth crushed them with his blood-stained
hands.

The terror of Macbeth spread through the land
As the devil's puppet-king rode out
And slew the good, the kind, the innocent,
And stained the purple heather hellfire red.

But guilt and dreadful dreams began to haunt
His Lady as she tried to sleep each night.
She thought she saw the blood spots on her hands...
A sea of water would not wash it off.

As enemies drew near Macbeth's grey walls,
His guilt-mad lady tumbled from a tower
And killed herself. The soldier king, alone,
Went out to fight the rebels to the death.

Of course, he thought, the witches' demon power
Would shield him from the angry, slicing steel.
But witches from the devil can deceive
A man and drag his soul away to Hell.

And so it was, Macbeth faced his last fight,
Betrayed by witches, cackling in their den.
He stepped out on the blood-soaked plain and fought
And killed for he believed he'd never die.

Until a hero, blessed with magic power
As strong as King Macbeth's, strode out.
The brave Macduff was seeking to avenge
The murder of his helpless wife and child.

Macbeth was weary of the blood and grief,
He knew now that this fight would be his last.
So King Macbeth came face to face with death
And welcomed it as if it were his friend.

The son of murdered Duncan claimed the throne
Of Scotland and at least the Scots knew peace.
But somewhere, on the moors, beneath the
dripping rocks
The witches wait, and plot and weave their evil
charms.

Fillet of a fenny snake, in the cauldron boil and bake.
Eye of newt and toe of frog, wool of bat and tongue of
dog
Adder's fork and blind-worm's sting, lizard's leg, and
howlet's wing –
For a charm of powerful trouble, like a hell-broth, boil
and bubble.

Did you know....?

In 1590 James had heard there were witches in North Berwick who were plotting to kill him, through a witchcraft curse! Reports said that they had thrown cats and bits of dead human bodies into the North Sea as he was sailing across it. This raised a storm which almost wrecked James's ship.

James survived, heard of the plot and sent for the witches. He questioned their leader, Agnes Sampson. To his amazement the woman repeated to James some of the things he had whispered to his wife on the night of his wedding – words that no one but James and Anne could have heard.

The king believed he had survived because he was a rightful king and protected by God. Shakespeare took this idea of a rightful king and witchcraft and wove them into his play *Macbeth*.

FANTASTIC FACTS 9: THE MACBETH CURSE

Shakespeare's second most popular play is his shortest, perhaps because some of the scenes were lost before the play could be printed.

But it's not only popular because it's short! It's popular because it has all the things that interest audiences today just as they interested them in 1606 when it was written. Lots of murders, lots of blood, magical supernatural forces and powerful characters seeking justice and revenge.

The play Macbeth also looks at the subject of witchcraft. Over the past four hundred years actors have come to believe that any performance of the play stirs up the ancient spirits and can bring bad luck. They believe that Macbeth is cursed.

They are so superstitious that they will never say the name Macbeth while they are in a theatre, unless they are performing in it, of course. Instead they simply call it "The Scottish Play".

But are the actors right to fear the Macbeth curse? Do performances have a history of bad luck, danger, or even death?

Look at the facts and make up your own mind:

TARTAN TERRORS

1 *Macbeth* was written in 1606, so the curse struck early. On 7th August 1606 it is said that Hal Berridge, the boy-actor playing Lady Macbeth, died backstage during the performance.

2 In 1721 rich members of the audience were still allowed to sit on the stage. When one lord wandered across to talk to his friend on the other side, the actor playing Macbeth became upset. He drew his sword and attacked. The lord's friends defended him. Soon the actors were all fighting with the audience and drove them out onto the street. The rioters returned with more friends and wrecked the theatre. The army finally restored order and for a long time armed guards protected every performance.

3 There is a lot of fake blood splashed around in most productions of *Macbeth*. In an 1850s performance

Macbeth and Lady Macbeth missed the stage hand who was waiting with fresh water and a towel to rinse them off. They dashed to a dressing room, washed, and grabbed some cloth for a towel. They hurried back to the stage and threw the cloth in a corner. The next morning the manager was very upset: "There are thieves in the theatre! Mr Simkin's trousers were stolen from his dressing room." Macbeth and Lady Macbeth looked at one another but kept silent about the "cloth" they'd snatched the night before. "And to make it worse," the manager groaned, "Mr Simkin had to go home without any trousers and it was *snowing!*"

4 But Mr Simkin was lucky compared to a visitor at a Charles Macready performance. The visitor was thrilled that he was allowed to stand at the side of the stage and watch Macready play *Macbeth*. Macready rushed off the stage and looked for the stage hand who was supposed to be holding a dish of fake blood. The man and the blood were missing! Macready saw the visitor, raised his fist and smashed the poor man in the nose. Soon he had all the blood he needed for the scene – real blood!

5 In 1882 a witch's cat put in an appearance on stage. It strolled on the stage, looking for mice, in the middle of Macbeth's most dramatic speech. The audience fell about laughing. Macbeth helped the cat off the stage with his boot. A big mistake. But it was no laughing matter when the sword fight then went wrong. Macduff was supposed to thrust his sword under Macbeth's arm. In fact he thrust it straight into his chest and wounded him severely. The revenge of the cat, perhaps?

6 There is a scene in *Macbeth* where three murderers attack Macbeth's friend Banquo. In a US production the actor playing the Third Murderer got a little carried away and thrust a dagger into Banquo's ear. The actor survived. But was the Third Murderer too keen or too cursed?

7 A 1934 production had four actors playing *Macbeth* in a single week. Number 1, Malcolm Keen lost his voice. Number 2, Alistair Sim, fell ill with a heavy chill. Number 3 was sacked after an argument with the company manager. Actor Number 4, John Laurie, survived.

8 In 1948 actress Diane Wynyard made the mistake of saying she didn't believe in the curse. She made a second mistake by insisting that she play Lady Macbeth's sleep-walking scene with her eyes closed. "Sleep-walkers always have their eyes closed," she said. She walked along the battlements of Macbeth's castle with her eyes closed, walked off the edge and fell five metres (fifteen feet). The battered actress picked herself up and finished the performance, cursing her clumsiness, no doubt!

9 Not even audiences are safe from the curse. In the 1938 Stratford production an elderly man parked his car at the theatre and set off to see the play. Then he heard a rushing sound and turned in time to see his parked car running down the hill towards him. He was too old to jump out of the way and the car rolled over him, crushing his legs. That seems to have been a car-cursed *Macbeth*. Lady Macbeth ran hers into a shop window. The actor playing Macduff should have been safe. He had to arrive on stage on a horse, but he fell off and injured himself seriously. Horse-play can be dangerous.

10 In 1935 an African company played *Macbeth* in New York and used spells from ancient tribal rituals to *protect* them from the curse. A real witch-doctor was said to have sacrificed four black goats to help with the spell. It seemed to work. The play was a great success. But one newspaper reporter said it was "an exhibition of boondoggling"– it was rubbish! When the cast heard of this report they were upset – their chants changed from "protecting" to "cursing". The newspaper reporter fell ill and within a few days he was dead. He died of pneumonia, some people said.

Compared to these disasters the usual stage accidents seem small. Like the parade of eight ghostly kings in Act IV. In an 1850 London performance king one dropped his crown and, as he bent down to pick it up, king two bumped into the back of him and the eight kings piled up on stage like falling dominoes. Some ghoulish members of the audience go to performances of *Macbeth* in the hope of seeing some disasters. That night they went home happy!

SORRY FELLAS!

STORY 10: HAMLET

Of all Shakespeare's plays *Hamlet* is probably the most famous. It has been performed all over the world in hundreds of languages. Books have been written about it – more books than about any other play or novel.

Hamlet's famous line, "To be, or not to be: that is the question," is known by most people – people who couldn't quote another word from Shakespeare's plays.

Hamlet has everything Elizabethan audiences loved. It's a murder story, it's a ghost story, it's a love story and it's a mystery. There are sword fights, hauntings, comic scenes and even a mime play within the play. But it began as the greatest Elizabethan favourite – a revenge play. The curious thing is that it takes Hamlet the *whole play* to get that revenge. It's not so much a "revenge" play as a "not-revenge-just-yet" play!

There are so many deaths that it would take a whole police department to work out who did what to whom. If a policeman did have to write an account of the deaths, then his report would make fascinating reading...

The topped ten

"It's the most baffling case we've ever had to deal with," the chief inspector said. "Bodies all over the place."

"That's awful, sir," I agreed.

"Awful! It's a disaster! Think of all the paperwork we'll have to deal with. It will take us weeks, months!"

"Years?" I nodded looking at the twisted bodies sprawled over the castle floor. There was at least one king, one queen and a prince not to mention assorted courtiers and a skeleton of unknown origin.

Every time there's a murder case we have to fill in a Form 2B and it takes hours. The inspector leaned forward and breathed onion breath in my face. "Try to arrange it so there are no 2B forms to fill in," he hissed. Then he was gone.

I walked over to a man sitting in a corner of the castle hall. He was wrapped in a black cloak. "Name?" I demanded.

"Horatio," he moaned.

"Well, Mr Horatio, I arrest you in the name of the law."

He blinked and looked up at me. "Me? Why me?"

"Because you're the only one left alive," I snapped. Then I remembered a murder arrest meant filling in a 2B form. I was hoping he could come up with a good explanation.

"I can come up with a good explanation," he said. I gave a huge sigh of relief.

"Sit on this chair," I ordered. "Explain."

As he sat on it, I handcuffed his ankle to the leg of the chair. An old trick they taught me in the Danish police training school.

"It all began on a freezing, moonless midnight," he said.

"It often does, sir," I nodded.

"The guards were patrolling the walls of Elsinore Castle here when they reported seeing a ghost."

"Drunk?" I asked.

"No, the ghost was quite sober!" Horatio insisted.

"I meant the guards! Oh, never mind. Get on with it."

"It sounded like the ghost of the old king, Hamlet. I went and told his son, Hamlet..."

I was beginning to make notes. I stopped. "I thought the king was Hamlet."

"He was."

"But you said the prince was Hamlet."

"He was."

"They were both called Hamlet?" I checked.

"They were."

"Just checking. Carry on."

"Prince Hamlet was my friend at university. I told him about the ghost and he came out onto the battlements to see for himself. The ghost of King Hamlet told his son that he had been poisoned..."

"Murdered?" I gasped.

"Murdered," Horatio agreed. "King Hamlet had been sleeping in an orchard. His brother, Claudius, dripped poison into his ear and killed him."

"Ah, but a ghost can't give evidence at a trial," I grinned. No forms to fill in for this one. "Murder by person or persons unknown."

Horatio scowled at me. "The evil Claudius was the one who gained by King Hamlet's death," he pointed out. "He took the throne and he married the queen Gertrude, King Hamlet's widow and Prince Hamlet's mother."

"He married three women!" I gasped.

"They were all the same woman," Horatio snapped. "No wonder the ghost of the king couldn't rest!"

"The ghost wanted to kill Claudius?" I guessed.

"No ... the ghost wanted his son, Prince Hamlet, to kill Claudius."

"The royal avenger," I breathed. "Very noble."

"Unfortunately, my friend Hamlet was no murderer. He couldn't kill anyone in cold blood. His excuse was that the ghost could have been a devil, not the true ghost of his father."

"Very wise," I said. "Can't go around killing people just 'cos a ghost tells you to!"

"So Hamlet set a trap," Horatio went on. "He hired a group of actors to perform a play in which a king is murdered by his brother by dripping poison in his ear. The play was performed in front of Claudius, and you should have seen him panic! That's when Hamlet knew his uncle was a murderer."

"So, he killed him," I sighed.

"Not yet. He had a chance when Claudius was praying in church, but Hamlet let him escape. Instead he went to shout at his mother for marrying Claudius. Unfortunately, old Polonius (he was responsible for running the royal houshold) was hiding behind a curtain in the queen's room. Hamlet saw the curtain move, thought it was Claudius and stabbed through the curtain. Killed old Polonius in an instant."

I thought about it for a moment. "That's two dead," I said. "But stabbing a man like that is accidental death, not murder," I said.

"Unfortunately, Polonius's daughter, Ophelia, was in love with Hamlet. The killing drove her mad. She drowned herself."

"Three gone," I blinked. "Suicide is punishable by death. But since she drowned, we needn't bother with her."

"I'm not so sure about that," Horatio said quickly. "Her brother, Laertes, was furious. Prince Hamlet had killed his father..."

"Accidentally," I pointed out.

"Accidentally, and brought about the death of his sister..."

"By suicide."

"Laertes was determined to kill Hamlet."

"Not another murder," I groaned.

"Not yet. Hamlet wasn't in Denmark at the time. Claudius had hired two men, Rosencrantz and Guildenstern, to take Hamlet on a trip to England. Claudius sent a secret letter to the king of England asking him to kill Prince Hamlet as soon as he landed," Horatio explained.

"But he survived?"

"Hamlet switched the letter for another one that asked the English to kill Rosencrantz and Guildenstern instead. They did!"

I made a note. "That's five dead so far. But Rosencrantz and Guildenstern are England's problem, not mine," I said, relieved.

"Hamlet survived and came back to Denmark," Horatio went on. "King Claudius then planned to have Hamlet killed in a duel."

"Fair fight. That's not murder," I said quickly.

"It is murder when the king planned to give Laertes a poisoned sword and give Hamlet a poisoned drink, just to make sure!" the young man argued.

I shrugged. "Sounds like a family matter to me, not a case for the police. But carry on. What happened?"

"Hamlet came back from England in time to see Ophelia's grave being dug. The grave diggers found a skull..."

"No!" I cried. "That's number six!"

"It was the skull of the old court jester, Yorick."

"Don't tell me he was murdered!" I moaned.

"No, he died of old age, years ago."

I wiped my brow. "Phew. That's good. I'm running out of paper here," I complained.

"Laertes turned up at Ophelia's funeral and almost killed Hamlet on the spot. They were wrestling in the grave and had to be torn apart!"

"Very muddy, grave-wrestling," I said sadly. "Shouldn't be allowed."

"Anyway," Horatio went on, "Laertes and Hamlet appeared before Claudius and Queen Gertrude for their duel."

"With a poisoned sword?"

Horatio nodded. "And poisoned wine."

"Somebody could get hurt there," I said.

The young man looked at the pile of bodies behind me.

"So what happened?" I asked and turned my paper over. I was having to write on the back now and my pencil needed sharpening.

"Hamlet and Laertes fought and Laertes wounded Hamlet. The poison began to work. But then the swords fell from their hands, they got mixed up and Hamlet was fighting with the poisoned sword. He stabbed Laertes and Laertes began to die!"

"Nasty," I said.

"Then Queen Gertrude drank the poisoned wine by mistake and she began to die. She warned Hamlet about the poison. Then she died!"

"That's number seven, I reckon. Died of drinking wine, did she? We'll put that one down as food poisoning, I think."

"Hamlet was furious," Horatio went on. "He realized he was dying, so he stabbed Claudius and forced him to drink the rest of the poisoned wine."

"Sounds fair enough to me," I chuckled. "He was a nasty piece of work, that Claudius!"

"He died."

"Number eight!" I laughed. "If he drank the

wine and knew it was poisoned, I guess we can call that another suicide."

"Then Laertes died from the poisoned sword..."

"Number nine! We'll put that one down as blood poisoning, I think. That's what happens when you fight with a rusty sword!" I laughed again. I could see there would be no 2B murder forms for me to fill in! "We're nearly in double figures here! Go on, finish the story."

Horatio looked very sour, I have to say. In fact there was a tear in the corner of his eye as he said, "And finally, of course, my friend Hamlet died from the poisoned sword." He buried his face in his cloak and wept.

I put my pencil away. "That's ten. All topped! A sort of topped ten! Any more you want to tell me about?"

He shook his head and groaned. I decided not to arrest him and I left him to get on with it. He had a lot of funerals to arrange.

I was more interested in getting back to the boss with the news that there did not seem to be any murder cases there to investigate and, most important, none of those great, thick, boring 2B murder forms to fill in. I knew as soon as I walked into his office what the first thing he'd say to me would be. And I was right.

"2B or not 2B? That is the question!"

Did you know...?

Hamlet was such a popular play it was performed by anyone wanting to attract a large audience. It was even performed in the nineteenth century by clowns and pantomime artists. Their favourite stunt was to use a performing dog to add fun to the play. Hamlet's dog was trained to keep an eye on wicked Claudius and, at the end of the play, to rip out the throat of the king! These popular, hilarious Hamlets became known as "Dog Hamlets".

FANTASTIC FACTS 10: QUICK QUIZ

Here are a few facts about Shakespeare and his theatre. But which are true and which are false?

Foul and funny facts

1 Shakespeare's plays used special effects like dummy heads that could be cut off. True/false?

2 Each company had a "tireman" whose job was to make sure the wheels on the travelling carts were kept in good repair. True/false?

3 Plays were usually followed by a comic dance. True/false?

4 In Shakespeare's play *The Tempest* a feast was made to vanish to show the magician's power. True/false?

5 Shakespeare wrote the play *Cardenio*. True/false?

6 Shakespeare re-wrote his plays many times and wasted a lot of paper. True/false?

7 The part of King Hamlet's ghost was played by William Shakespeare himself. True/false?

8 Shakespeare made extra money when his poems (The Sonnets) were published in 1609. True/false?

9 *The Merry Wives of Windsor* was the only play

Shakespeare wrote about his own time and his own country. True/false?

10 Shakespeare's bloodiest play is probably *Titus Andronicus*. Titus cuts up two boys and serves them in a pie for their mother to eat. True/false?

Answers:

1 True. Macbeth has his head cut off and held up for the audience to cheer. In *Henry VI* a character enters with an arrow through his neck. Animal blood would often be used to wet the hands of murderers in the plays. In a Christopher Marlowe play devils ran around the stage with fireworks in their mouths.

2 False. The tireman looked after the costumes of the actors: their "attire".

3 True. Even after a tragic play the actors would try to send the audience home with smiles on their faces. The dancers would move through the audience and collect money in hats.

4 True. The feast was set on a round board. A character was "flown" over the stage on ropes. As the audience looked up to watch, the table top was flipped over to

show a bare board. When the audience looked back the feast had magically vanished!

5 True. This play is the only one known to be written by Shakespeare but totally lost. In the eighteenth century Bishop Warburton said he owned a copy of *Cardenio* but his cook Betsy used it to light the fire. If *you* ever find a copy *don't* use it to light a fire. It would be worth millions of pounds today.

6 False. Shakespeare was well-known for being a careful writer. He had to be. A single sheet of paper cost more than a loaf of bread. Work out how much that would be at today's prices.

7 True. The ghost would have appeared through a trap-door in the stage and popped up to terrify the audience. We also know that Shakespeare played the part of Gloucester (who had his eyes gouged out) in *King Lear*.

8 False. Shakespeare's poems were somehow stolen and printed without his permission. The printer made money from them but Shakespeare didn't.

9 True. There is a story that Shakespeare wrote it because Queen Elizabeth asked him to. That's unlikely. But it is true that he finished it in just three weeks.

10 True. They had already cut out the tongue and cut off the hands of Lavinia to silence her, so it served the boys right. Lavinia, by the way, wrote the names of her attackers in the sand with a stick.

EPILOGUE

Shakespeare has been called the most successful writer of all time. He was more than that. He was an actor and a theatre manager and a poet. He was a success in all of them.

Thanks to Shakespeare we have a richer English language. Thanks to Shakespeare we have many fine theatres today. Theatre was very young when Shakespeare started working in it. Without a powerful and popular writer to draw in thousands of people it might not have survived. If they hadn't seen plays they enjoyed, the Elizabethans would have gone back to their bear-baiting and cock-fighting for entertainment.

The sign of a great writer is that their work survives beyond their lifetime. Shakespeare has not only survived four hundred years but he has survived so many attempts to make him *boring*. Academics have taken him so seriously that they almost made us forget that Shakespeare wrote to *entertain*.

But perhaps from these ten best stories you can understand how enjoyable his plays can be. There are many other great Shakespeare stories which didn't make this top ten, of course. Read them as stories, read them as plays, see them on video, see them at the cinema or (best of all) try to see them live on stage. Make up your own mind about which one is your favourite. Which would be your number one?

If we can remember his exciting stories, fascinating characters and wonderful words, then he will certainly survive another 400 or 4,000 years. He was not just a writer for the Elizabethan stage or the Elizabethan age. His friend Ben Jonson explained it best when he said:

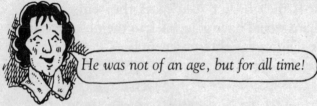

He was not of an age, but for all time!

Your time. Try to see his plays for yourself and laugh, cry, cheer or gasp at the drama.

He'd like that.

ENJOY !!!